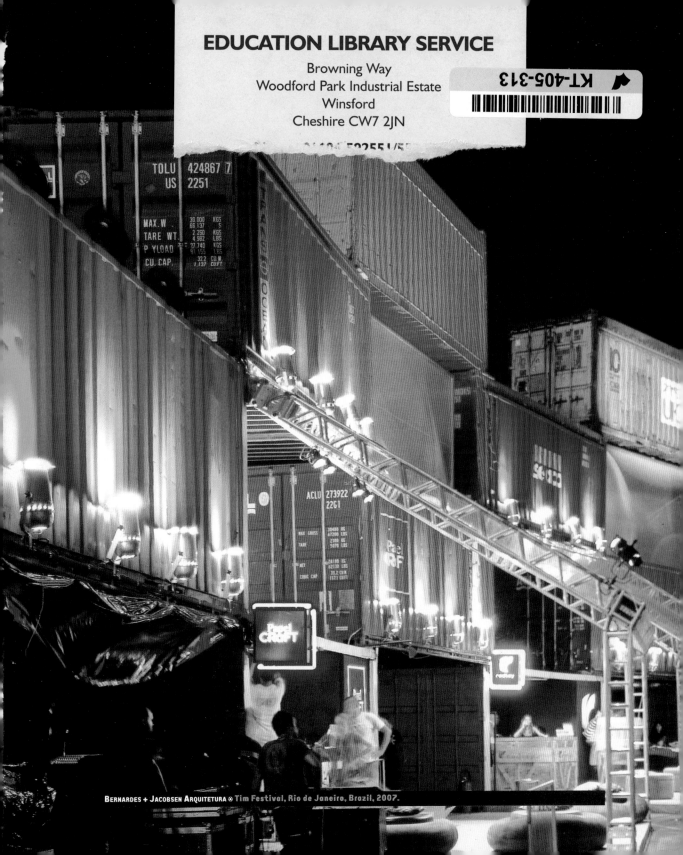

BERNARDES + JACOBSEN ARQUITETURA ✷ Tim Festival, Rio de Janeiro, Brazil, 2007.

CSCEC+PVVT+CCDI AND ARUP ⊛ National Aquatics Center, Beijing, China, 2008.

JEAN-MARC IBOS AND MYRTO VITART ✴ Extension to the Palais des Beaux-Arts, Lille, France, 1997.

CHRISTIAN DE PORTZAMPARC ✹ Musée Hergé, Louvain-la-Neuve, Belgium, 2009.

ZAHA HADID, Chanel Mobile Art, Central Park, New York, 2007.

GILLES DE BURE

talk about contemporary architecture

Flammarion

CONTENTS

Dominique Perrault and Gaëlle Lauriot-Prévost ⊛ Mesh, architectonic metallic netting, 1995.

PREFACE

There is a first time for everything.
To be ten years old and to stumble upon the Place des Vosges in Paris—on the cusp of the 1950s when it was still cobbled, furrowed, wrinkled, almost dilapidated, and not yet papered over by its tidy little square—is to be captivated, dazzled, carried away without knowing why or how. An unforgettable experience.

Especially when I was as yet blissfully unaware of the existence of the word "architecture." Later, much later, Claude-Nicolas Ledoux, the sublime architect of the equally sublime Saline Royale, the royal saltworks at Arc-et-Senans, was to provide the key: "Architecture enfolds the beholder in the beguilement of the marvelous."

Over time there were to be many more encounters of no less intensity. In Paris at first, with the baroque wonders of the chapel of Val-de-Grâce and the classical splendor of the Palais de l'Institut, soon followed by (in no particular order) the temple at Abu Simbel, the Pantheon and the Villa Medici in Rome, the Great Mosque in Cordoba and the Alhambra in Granada, the Temple of Heaven in Beijing and the Zen gardens of Kyoto, the fortress of Sigiriya in Sri Lanka and palaces of Abomey in Benin, Sinan's domes in Istanbul and the pyramids in the Yucatan, neoclassical visions in Bath and baroque vistas in Bratislava, the walls of Taroudant and Vauban's enceintes.

"It was," as Bakunin proclaimed, "a feast without beginning or end!" Then came—pell-mell once more—modern and contemporary works. After all, to leap from the Yemeni "skyscrapers" at Sana'a to a cast-iron building in Chicago is both delightful and revelatory. Others followed: the skylines of New York and Hong Kong; the Shanghai Bund and throwbacks to the Bauhaus in Tel Aviv; the ultra-contemporary "mini houses" somehow inserted into the gaps in the "teeth" of Tokyo and various dream houses in Finland, the United States, France, and Australia; London's rustic scenery and the big skies of Valparaiso; the vast esplanades of Saint Petersburg and the dust of Johannesburg; the canals of Venice and Amsterdam; the Moscow subway and various futuristic airports.

And everywhere bristles with architecture, with buildings that impose themselves (literally, as well as metaphorically), landmarks on a journey that nourishes or jogs the memory, arousing an emotional response, a sensation, giving pleasure or hinting at deeper mysteries. The eyes flit to and fro. The mind wanders far and wide.

"Tell me (since you are so sensibile to the effects of architecture), have you not noticed, in walking about this city, that among the buildings with which it is peopled, certain are *mute*, others *speak* and others, finally—and they are the most rare—*sing*?"* wrote Paul Valéry in *Eupalinos, or the Architect.*

A marvelous, peerless definition of architecture: an art which renders useless, null and void, perhaps, our notions of time and space.

Ancient, classical, modern, or contemporary, spontaneous or calculated, intuitive or conceptual—the plurality of architecture is one and indivisible, since it is an art, a creative act, a language. To understand it, one has to learn how to decipher these "books of stone," which (whatever their history or geography) form a timeless and universal storehouse—much like the "ideal library" of the Argentinian writer Jorge Luis Borges. There are so many absent friends, so many unresolved questions and blind spots, that trying to give an account of all our emotions, of all our discoveries—even if we limit ourselves to the contemporary era—is simply impossible. Even if one is prepared to make the sacrifice and classify them by function, purpose, or style, the job is no less onerous. To reveal their personality and singularity, their autonomy and difference, shorn of context, is—to use a favorite expression of Jean Clair and Harald Szeemann—to exhibit a collection of "bachelor machines**."

There is a first time for everything, certainly. But, if the desire, the curiosity, and the enthusiasm remain intact, then every time can be a first time.

GILLES DE BURE

* Selected writings of Paul Valéry,
New Directions, NY, 1990, p. 175.
** Term first used in 1913 by Marcel Duchamp
to describe elements of his work *Large Glass.*

REJECT/ACCEPT?

In every period, under every climate, resistance to progress, invention, and imagination, to the fluctuations or evolutions of language (whether in literature, music, art, cinema, dance, or poetry) is an almost universal constant. Architecture, as an art that impacts everyone, is particularly prone to such reactions. Yet it is easy to forget that our resistance is based in turn on comparisons and contrasts with whatever happens to constitute the prevailing architectural heritage. It fails to take into account that this very heritage aroused, in its time, the very same resistance, rejection, and dismissal. Moreover, it fails to see that these "jewels of the past" have all, in their time, been instrumental to "progress."

"Whatever comes into the world and disturbs nothing deserves neither consideration nor patience," wrote the French poet René Char. Georges Bataille, meanwhile, drove home the point : "Limits exist solely so they can be surpassed."

Heightening our senses, widening our horizons: this is perhaps the very essence of architecture. Especially since—most of the time—rejection is followed by acceptance. In 1887, in Paris, the Eiffel Tower was inaugurated for the Universal Exhibition. Almost immediately, an artists' manifesto was published in the newspaper *Le Temps* on February 14, and signed by, among others, Alexandre Dumas *fils*, Charles Garnier, the architect of the Paris Opera, and poets François Coppée, Leconte de Lisle, and Sully Prudhomme. "We come," it bellowed, "writers, painters, sculptors, architects, passionate lovers of the hitherto unpolluted beauty of Paris, to protest with all our strength, with all our indignation, in the name of French taste, in the name of French art and history here under threat, against the erection, in the very heart of our capital, of the pointless and monstrous Eiffel Tower." One signatory of the pamphlet, Guy de Maupassant, who often dined in the Tower ("because it is the only place from which it cannot be seen"), was so outraged by the structure that the artists' diatribe was dubbed the "Maupassant Manifesto."

Another writer, Léon Bloy, called the Tower a "tragic lamppost." Today the Eiffel Tower, the preeminent symbol of Paris, is visited by nearly 7 million paying customers a year: that is to say it has become the most visited monument of its kind in the world.

Ninety years later, in 1977, on the day before its opening, a dense crowd gathered in front of the Centre Pompidou. No pamphlet this time, but a rolling series of demonstrations, to the point that staff at the center were seriously worried and scaled the temporary barriers to take refuge in the building. Beyond its walls, the word that cropped up most frequently was "Meccano." Until one wiseacre, who had probably not yet come to terms with the Eiffel Tower, quipped: "After the derrick, here's the refinery." And yet, just as with Eiffel's structure, over the following days people came in droves to the center to explore, discover, and, perhaps, to give themselves the time and opportunity to get to like it.

Examples of this kind abound, landmarks in the history of architecture. Like Paris, San Francisco boasts two examples of rejection–acceptance of its own. At the time of its construction (1933–37) the Golden Gate Bridge was the subject of a chorus of disapproval; in 1972 William L. Pereira's Transamerica Pyramid also aroused violent opposition. And yet today, both bridge and tower are twin symbols of San Francisco. As the American filmmaker John Huston, who knew a thing or two about life, was fond of saying: "Politicians, whores, and ugly buildings all get respectable if they last long enough."

1

DID YOU SAY CONTEMPORARY ARCHITECTURE?

WHEN DID IT ALL BEGIN?

If it's possible to pin an exact date on such developments, *it* all started, unquestionably, in the 1970s. The telltale signs came thick and fast in the first half of the decade, snowballed during the second, and finally crystallized in various forms over the following years. But before analyzing its diverse expressions, we should start with a little history.

Four-and-a-half centuries before the onset of the Christian calendar, the Greek Anaxagoras of Clazomenae, while he was not pondering the squaring of the circle, came up with a hitherto unrecognized truth: "Nothing is lost, nothing is created, everything changes." This statement was repeated many centuries later by the chemist Antoine Lavoisier to whom, indeed, it is commonly ascribed.

That is to say that, in architecture as in any other creative field, invention, imagination, and progress flow into one another in a seamless continuum—rather than against the shifting background of revolution or in an eternal battle between ancients and moderns.

"The architect, like the poet, is a creator who confronts threadbare values that have lost their dynamism with new ones ripe for the picking," as the historian Denise Basdevant puts it.

One thinks back to Prince Salina in Lampedusa's *The Leopard* when he murmurs: "Everything has to change so that nothing changes." Both quotations stress the fact that, despite the bandying about of words like "step change," we should talk rather about stages, about landmarks along the road of art, of thought, which unfold logically in time and space. Still, this does not mean we can't acknowledge the milestones.

"Modern" architecture as such came into being in 1920–30, its development and expansion being brutally cut short by the Second World War. The immediate postwar period had to devote itself not to architecture, but to reconstruction, to hasty, sometimes thoughtless rebuilding, promoted by new materials and techniques, by prefabrication, and by model theory.

And then, suddenly, smack in the middle of the 1960s, the situation improved visibly. The West was on the cusp of decades of post-baby boom expansion, the economy was getting back on its feet, optimism was no longer laughable, the horizon brightened, and experimentation was once again in the air.

As the years progressed, harbingers included the construction ex nihilo of sites such as Le Corbusier's Chandigarh in India and Lúcio Costa and Oscar Niemeyer's Brasilia. The majority of Western nations were unsurprised to see polemical structures springing up in which didacticism and technique, expression and materials, art and function were inextricably intertwined.

In 1972, Frei Otto delivered an Olympic stadium in Munich whose tensile structures made of synthetic fiber became the envy of the world. Meanwhile in Paris, Roger Taillibert was constructing the Parc des Princes stadium—a tour de force of technology, certainly, but also, and above all, one of form. In the following year, 1973, the American architect Minoru Yamasaki sent the Twin Towers of the World Trade Center soaring up from the tip of Manhattan, while the Dane Jørn Utzon was to set gliding over the waters of the port of Sydney his astonishing Opera House. In these two buildings economic power and cultural vigor were embodied in two symbols of massive impact.

In 1974, in Dacca, Bangladesh, the American Louis Kahn erected the most

severe incarnation conceivable of political might with his awe-inspiring and splendid National Assembly building. The same year, with the new Paris airport built on the wide plain of Roissy-en-France, Paul Andreu's masterly composition strove to solve the increasingly urgent problem of passenger flow.

At the end of the decade, and against all expectation considering French conservatism, it was Paris that was to provide two particularly successful examples of contemporary architecture; one opulent and headline-grabbing, the other more modest yet no less universal.

Renzo Piano and Richard Rogers, Centre Pompidou, Paris, France, 1977. If contemporary architecture can be said to date from one building, it would be without question the Centre Pompidou whose opening produced a shock wave.

On February 1, 1977, the Centre Pompidou opened its doors to the public. Designed by an Italian, Renzo Piano, and an Englishman, Richard Rogers, it became a symbol of the future of the cultural venue and kicked off what became known as the high-tech style. Two years later, in the thirteenth arrondissement, the French architect Christian de Portzamparc inaugurated Les Hautes Formes, a residential unit in which he put into practice his theory of the *îlot ouvert* (the open block). Although few Parisians are aware of its existence, architects from around the world flock to see it.

DOES IT HAVE TO BE SPECTACULAR AND/OR MONUMENTAL?

Architecture sometimes, even often, resembles the visual arts. With very little effort, minimal art, conceptual art, or land art can arouse an emotional upsurge. Similarly, architecture has increasingly tended to shed its weight, its permanence, its heaviness, opting instead, as often as it can, for the immaterial, for emptiness, silence, for the "almost nothing," to set up a subtle dialectical interplay between presence and absence, appearance and disappearance, and relationships based on adhesion rather than on hindrance.

This tendency, this striving for nothingness, is often manifested in works of great richness and great complexity, creating worlds that are infinite, paradoxical, impalpable—whether they are born from chance (from inspiration?) or from (budgetary) necessity.

Very frequently, it is in "small forms," or minor projects, that the architect's imagination comes into its own. With its relatively small territory and constantly swelling population, Japan is familiar with this state of affairs. Living space is at a premium and, consequently, any gaps there are have to be filled.

Thus, in 2003, the architect Kinya Maruyama came to design an extension for the Hikari crèche in Yuri Honjou. Lack of space, restricted budget, tight deadline. The result: a multipurpose hall, a pocket theater whose shape floats between kite, cockscomb, kneeling samurai, and mythical bird with outspread wings. There, on a shoestring budget, Maruyama produced a minor masterpiece of poetry and humor that mixes the complexity of the game of go with a Surrealist cast of mind (allusions to the "exquisite corpse"), a penchant for utopia with a sensibility for nature.

In 2005 Terunobu Fujimori built a *chashitsu tetsu* (teahouse) in the Kiyoharu Shirakaba Museum of Art in Yamanashi, Japan, a hut leaning against a cypress and overlooking a stand of cherry trees. The cypress stump passes straight through the hut like a spinal column and plays the role of a stabilizer in the event of typhoon or earthquake. Though generously open to the outside in order to make the most of the scenery and the cherry blossom, rather than folded in on itself as it tradition would have it, this house of tea can be read as a tribute to the famous "Golden Tearoom," also built in a tree by the sixteenth-century architect, Rikyu. Thus can respect for tradition, memory,

Mobile Studio, Kinya Maruyama, extension of the Yuri Honjou crèche, Japan, 2005.

RIGHT

Terunobu Fujimori, teahouse, Tetsu Kiyoharu Shirakaba Museum of Art, Yamanashi, Japan, 2005.

Kawaii! The Japanese certainly have a sense of the "almost nothing," in the shape of a doll's house. But what links these two structures is their curious blend of humor and grace, of tradition and modernity, of economy of means and generosity of imagination.

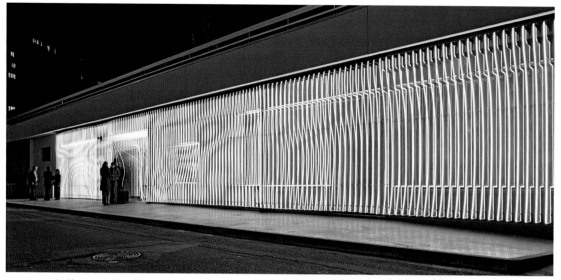

openness to the world, and a concern for the environment cohabit.

Along similar lines, memory of the past fuses with experimentation in the Santa Catarina market in Barcelona, renovated and enlarged by Enric Miralles and Benedetta Tagliabue in 2004, which extricates itself successfully from the existing building. Both open and covered, a long, undulating roof sits on a highly structured, uncompromising metal armature. The long wave bears a colorful pixelated composition in mosaic that is evocative of fruit and vegetables and, perhaps still more, of the famous mosaics in the Parc Güell, a masterpiece by the great Catalan architect, Antoni Gaudí.

About the same time in Boudry, Switzerland, a minimalist footbridge, comprising a structure made of slats of fir-wood and perfectly aligned branches thrown over the Areuse by the architects Geninasca and Delefortie, pays homage to both land art and arte povera: an aerial sculpture in the middle of a forest, of incomparable simplicity, lightness, and grace. Such examples of imaginative power combined with limited means and objectives proliferated—like Philippe Chiambaretta's spare facade for the Centre de Création Contemporaine in Tours, France.

Where mere "builders" will, in response to circumstances or constraints, overdo it, or else blindly pare down to a minimum, true architects, regardless of the problem faced or the means at their disposal, devote all their imagination, talent, genius, and energies to creating a work. "Give dancers slippers that are too small for them and they'll invent new steps," as the poet Paul Valéry suggested.

FACING PAGE, TOP
Philippe Chiambaretta/PCA, facade of the Centre de Création Contemporaine, Tours, France, 2007.

FACING PAGE, BOTTOM
Geninasca and Delefortrie, passageway over the Areuse, Boudry, Switzerland, 2002.

RIGHT
Rem Koolhaas, Villa Dall'Ava, Saint-Cloud, France, 1991.

Just the tiniest thing and everything else seems to make sense: with a few lines, Chiambaretta transcends the facade, while with a few subtly framed branches, Geninasca and Delefortrie turn their structure into something far more than a walkway, while a handful of featherlight pilotis is enough for Koolhaas to transform a building into a dreamscape.

ART, TECHNIQUE, OR MATERIALS?

On January 15, 1992, some time around 10:30 p.m., just as a lecture at the Centre Pompidou was drawing to a close, the French architect Jean Nouvel murmured, almost inaudibly, but with some feeling: "It should be the ambition of every architect to become a great artist. A hidden ambition, but a real one."

Yes, architecture is an art. And a major art at that, the most widely experienced, since it is the most visible, and can be entered and used by all. It is certainly an art, but not so simply defined. Auguste Perret, the architect of, among other things, the Théâtre des Champs-Élysées in Paris, an astonishing skyscraper in Amiens, and the rebuilt Le Havre (classified today by UNESCO as a World Heritage Site), expressed it in this way: "Architecture is the art of organizing space. It is expressed through construction." In this manner Perret distinguished architecture from construction, and design and creation from manufacture.

That is to say, the architect is an artist. But not only an artist.

Like a filmmaker who has to combine and coordinate a vast array of disciplines and professions, the architect, both loner and team player, has to be a designer, a manager, a technician, and a CEO. The Italian architect Renzo Piano provides an enlightening definition of his profession: "It is a pragmatic and highly complex trade. At 10 o'clock, you're a poet; at 11 o'clock a builder; and at noon a sociologist!" The task, obviously, is to give shape to all this poetry, creativity, thought, and expressivity.

All great architects have been confronted with the necessity of becoming great technicians. They need to be able to master technological advances, as well as new building techniques and materials; they need to be abreast of all such developments—and even keep one step ahead.

The phenomenal acceleration of science and technology today makes Le Corbusier's definition of architecture ("The masterly, correct, and magnificent play of volumes brought together in light") almost obsolete.

FACING PAGE, TOP
UNStudio, La Defense
Offices, Almere, The
Netherlands, 2003.

FACING PAGE, BOTTOM
Santiago Calatrava,
auditorium, Tenerife,
Spain, 2005.

RIGHT
Francis Soler and
Frédéric Druot,
Ministry of Culture,
Les Bons Enfants
site, Paris,
France, 2005.

Colored film between
two panes of glass,
structures that seem
to float in space,
metal lacework:
anything can be
expressed with
the right techniques
and materials.

Contemporary architecture is now realized in the context of the immaterial and the sustainable, rather than of the solid and the eternal.

For architecture today expresses itself more in terms of texture and tension than in terms of wall, rampart, and protection. Admittedly, stone, wood, glass, and metal are still present, but they are seconded by high-performance concrete, plastic derivatives, bamboo, titanium, and textiles, which are considered reactive, breathing elements, and generally treated as interfaces between inside and out.

Lattices, membranes, meshes, scales, braids, plates, plaques, honeycombs, and bubbles are no longer enclosures, but more like skins. Sometimes arborescent, sometimes evanescent, these skins can be screen-printed or pixelated, or covered in peroxide or plants.

Whether in cardboard for Shigeru Ban (emergency shelter in Kobe), zinc for Massimiliano Fuksas (the Candie project in Paris), titanium for Frank O. Gehry (the Bilbao Guggenheim), or in the form of greenery for Jean Nouvel (musée du quai Branly, Paris), mesh for Dominique Perrault (the Casa Majica in Madrid), wood (at the Centre Culturel Tjibaou in Nouméa, New Caledonia), earth for Renzo Piano (buildings in Berlin), or screen-printed glass for Francis Soler (buildings in Paris), these technical skins, in various materials, often double- or triple-thick, in addition to defining and determining a form, a style, an expression, play a role in the search for climatic or ecological balance.

Since art and technology are inseparable, the architect needs to keep abreast of current scientific and technological advances, to be on the cutting edge of research ("to remain immobile means to submit," Goethe had already written centuries ago), to experiment, to push boundaries. But scrutinizing a particular architectural variant under the microscope, poring over the ways and means of architecture, will tell us nothing about its creative unconscious or its artistic dimension. For it is receptivity more than cognition, perception more than knowledge, that determines emotion, feeling, and comprehension.

Who really cares how the temple at Abu Simbel in Egypt, Machu Picchu in Peru, the Taj Mahal in India, the Great Wall of China, or Palladio's Rotonda in Italy were *built*? It is the art, literature, musicality, and symbolism they harbor that have bestowed historical value on them and enabled them to stand the test of time.

ABOVE
Sarah Wigglesworth and Jeremy Till, house made of straw and sandbags, London, United Kingdom, 2001.

FACING PAGE
R&Sie, I'm Lost in Paris, experimental laboratory, Paris, France, 2008.

Traditional methods and timeless materials combine perfectly with contemporary economic and ecological awareness.

IS THE ARCHITECT A BRAND?

And the race is on! Entering competitions is, of course, a legitimate strategy for any architect who wants to express himself, to impose his "brand" internationally, and to develop his practice. National awards that consecrate a career or a specific structure abound, but there are three of global stature that dwarf them all, a triad of much-coveted, hoped-for awards that are the focus of intense lobbying.

The Pritzker Architecture Prize (considered the Nobel Prize of architecture) was founded in 1979 by Jay A. Pritzker through the Hyatt Foundation and carries a purse of one hundred thousand US dollars. **The Praemium Imperiale,** founded in 1988 on the occasion of the one hundredth anniversary of the Japan Art Association, is presented under the aegis of the Japanese Imperial family and worth some fifteen million yen. There are also awards for other disciplines (painting, sculpture, music, cinema). The lucky winner of **the European Union Prize for Contemporary Architecture Mies van der Rohe Award** founded in 1987 by the European Union and the Fundació Mies van der Rohe of Barcelona pockets sixty thousand euros. Three prizes, the first two fully international and the third confined to the borders of Europe; three prizes that are to architecture what the Cannes Film Festival, the Oscars, and the Venice Film Festival are to cinema or the World Cup, the Olympic Games, and the UEFA European Football Championship are to soccer.

"To those that have, it shall be given," or so the saying goes. For an architect to win one, or in some cases, several, of these prizes, means they has arrived, that they will be written about, celebrated, invited, commissioned. Hence their importance. And even if over the centuries fame has always brought success, in this time of intense personalization, in our "celebrity culture," the stakes are higher still.

Hence the need for an architect to combine a professional career with an active, headline-grabbing, social life. Hence the need to have a nose for handling the media and thus be published in the right specialist magazines and reviews, now joined by the near obligation to have one's face in the general-interest press. To make the cover of *Time* or *Paris-Match* certainly does no harm to the ego, but it is even more necessary if the agency is to make money. Today more than ever before, nights on the town, "doing" lunch, and appearing at cultural or business events have become part and parcel of the trade. Thus, in this steady stream of get-togethers, networks are built up and consolidated.

The major international competitions are must-do events and are all part of the game, whether one is invited as a competitor or as a member of the jury.

Moreover, all the prizes, media exposure, and competitions are monopolized by the same names, all of whom come from nations that have historically been architectural powerhouses: the German Otto Steidle; the Americans Frank O. Gehry, Thom Mayne, and Richard Meier; William Alsop, Norman Foster, and Richard Rogers from Britain; the Spaniards Santiago Calatrava and Rafael Moneo; the Frenchmen Jean Nouvel, Dominique Perrault, and Christian de Portzamparc; the Dutchman Rem Koolhaas; the Italians Massimiliano Fuksas and Renzo Piano; the Japanese Tadao Ando, Shigeru Ban, and SANAA; the Portuguese Álvaro Siza; the Swiss Herzog & de Meuron; not forgetting a Franco-Swiss resident of New York, Bernard Tschumi; and the British–Iraqi Zaha Hadid.

Yes, reluctantly, but wholly consciously, an architect is bound to become a brand name. Though this does not stop him possessing the talent or genius characteristic of any creative person.

One last distinguishing feature: black clothes. Men in black (and women, too, starting with Odile Decq, Zaha Hadid, and Kazuyo Sejima from SANAA): though they may brighten their dark suits and shirts with a long white or red scarf. Some even make a daredevil leap of imagination and swap black for charcoal gray.

ABOVE

Philip Johnson is, with Le Corbusier, one of the few architects to have had the honor of appearing on the cover of Time.

RIGHT

Kengo Kuma, LVMH Building, Osaka, Japan, 2004.

A handful of architects have become brands, stars. The media champions that often appear in the pages of news and celebrity magazines include: Frank O. Gehry, Norman Foster, Jean Nouvel, Zaha Hadid, and Tadao Ando. It is hardly surprising then to see that one of them, Kengo Kuma, has crowned the building he has built for a very grand company with a star.

A MAN'S JOB?

More often than seems fair, it is women who design and construct shelters, huts, yurts, wigwams, and igloos. But the architect's trade long remained an all-male preserve.

Of course, historians lay stress on the part played by Catherine Briçonnet in the construction of her château at Chenonceau in the sixteenth century; on the structural revolution initiated in the seventeenth century by the Marquise de Rambouillet in her *hôtel particulier* in Paris; on the interchange between Madame de Pompadour and Claude-Nicolas Ledoux in the design of the Petit Trianon in Versailles in the eighteenth century. In the twentieth century, the influence of Edith Farnsworth on her glass house by Mies van der Rohe; of Sarah Stein and Gabrielle de Monzie on the Villa Stein-de-Monzie built by Le Corbusier in Vaucresson; and that of Truus Schröder on her house designed by Gerrit Rietveld, are now accepted facts. Similarly acknowledged, after a period in the shadows, is the influence of Aino Marsio on the work of Alvar Aalto, Lily Reich on Mies van der Rohe, Charlotte Perriand on Le Corbusier, and Denise Scott Brown on Robert Venturi.

Yet one had to wait until 1890 for the first two architectural diplomas to be awarded to women, Signe Hornborg of Finland and the American Julia Morgan, students at the École des Beaux-Arts in Paris. They were followed by the Canadian Esther Marjorie Hill in Toronto in 1920 and the Swiss Flora Steiger-Crawford in Zurich in 1923.

In short, these were all exceptions that confirm the rule. But things were to change rapidly. All over the world, architectural schools now boast a female student population of almost 50 percent. Nevertheless, if the number of women architects is ever increasing, they tend to work in (mixed) duos or trios. For instance, there's the Japanese Kazuyo Sejima in SANAA; Benedetta Tagliabue in Barcelona (Miralles-

Tagliabue); the Frenchwomen Anne Lacaton (Lacaton-Vassal), Françoise N'Thépé (Beckmann-N'Thépé), and Myrto Vitar (Ibos and Vitar); the American Elizabeth Diller (Diller, Scofidio, Renfro); and the Dutchwomen Caroline Bos (UNStudio) and Nathalie de Vries (MVRDV).

Those who have managed to attain national or even international notoriety in a one-woman practice remain few and far between, despite the examples of the Italian Gae Aulenti, the Spaniard Carme Pinós, the Frenchwomen Odile Decq, Manuelle Gautrand, Françoise-Hélène Jourda, and Brigitte Métra, and of the Irano-British woman based in France, Nasrine Seraji.

The British-Iraqi Zaha Hadid, a figurehead of the deconstructivist movement and a global star—the only female winner to date of the Mies van der Rohe Prize (2003) and the Pritzker (2004)—is clearly ahead of the pack.

A MODE OF COMMUNICATION?

If architecture is primarily a form of expression, then, naturally, it has to speak, to sing, to tell a story. Sometimes, and increasingly so, it can also "communicate"—which is another thing entirely. In short, "identity"—both national and corporate—can benefit enormously from architecture seen as a particularly effective mode of "communication."

Two glaringly telltale examples illustrate this relationship: the Emirate of Abu Dhabi and the Vitra company. What is the purpose of the architectural fever that has seized the Gulf States in recent years? Or of the triumphant construction of *palazzi* in Venice, the mobile residences on the Princes' Island in Istanbul, or the swansong constituted by the Grand Projets as implemented by the President of the French Republic, François Mitterrand?

To understand Abu Dhabi, one has to approach the shores of the Persian Gulf with the work of a glorious quartet in mind; not Lawrence Durrell's *Alexandria Quartet*, of course, but the UAE version made up of Tadao Ando, Frank O. Gehry, Zaha Hadid, and Jean Nouvel. On the island of Saadiyat (the

"Island of Happiness") these four architects will, in the years to come, deliver a quartet of global cultural venues. Ando, a museum of the sea, a semi-immersed testament to the maritime realities of Abu Dhabi—shipping, trade, fishing, and piracy; Gehry is to build the largest Guggenheim Museum as an expression of his taste for interlocking forms and deconstruction; Hadid, a city of the arts with five theaters whose form will evoke the pearl oyster which was and which remains one of the sources of emirate's wealth; and finally Nouvel will be responsible for the Louvre Abu Dhabi, a dazzling interplay of light and shade topped with a vast dome casting its reflection in the water. Four major projects that testify to the fact that Abu Dhabi has chosen culture as its preferred channel of communication and as a theme for the development of tourism. These four major ventures will soon be joined by a fifth, the Sheikh Zayed National Museum currently being planned by Norman Foster.

Zaha Hadid, project for an arts center.

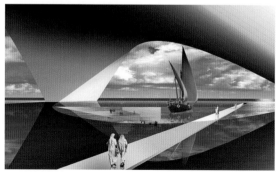

Tadao Ando, project for a museum dedicated to the sea.

Frank O. Gehry, project for the Guggenheim.

The Vitra company's venture is rather different, yet no less effective. The quality of the furniture and ensembles it produces, by some of the biggest names in international design (Charles and Ray Eames, Jean Prouvé, George Nelson, Verner Panton, Mario Bellini, Alberto Meda, Shiro Kuramata, Maarten van Severen, Ronan and Erwan Bouroullec, Philippe Starck), is widely appreciated. The same preoccupation with excellence appears when it turns to architecture.

Jean Nouvel, project for the Louvre.

Following a fire that partly destroyed its plant in 1981, Rolf Fehlbaum, the president of Vitra, wasted no time and went on the offensive. In Weil-am-Rhein, on the borders between Germany, Switzerland, and France, he inaugurated a building program of immense scale. With scarcely a pause for breath there sprung up three factories designed by Nicholas Grimshaw, Frank O. Gehry, and Álvaro Siza, a conference center by Tadao Ando, a museum of design by Gehry, and, in what was the first building built by the British-Iraqi architect, a fire station by Zaha Hadid. Five architects, five temperaments, five expressions that turned the site into a living museum of architecture, an impression reinforced by Fehlbaum's addition, at the entrance to the development, of one of the very first geodesic domes by the brilliant American architect and inventor Richard Buckminster Fuller, preserved intact in all its glory.

Two indubitable examples then of the dialectical and discursive presence of architecture which also show that when it comes to PR and commissions, architectural prizes are increasingly important, with the first and foremost being the Pritzker, considered the Nobel Prize of architecture. Our evidence? In Abu Dhabi, the five architects (Ando, Foster, Gehry, Hadid, and Nouvel) are all winners; at Weil-am-Rhein, four of the five (the odd-man-out is Grimshaw). The same applies to the foundations (Ando, Gehry, Herzog 8 de Meuron, Piano, Siza) and luxury storefronts (Hadid, Herzog 8 de Meuron, Koolhaas, Piano, Portzamparc, and there can be no doubt that Ito and SANAA will soon be awarded the prize, too).

FACING PAGE
Zaha Hadid,
fire station for
the Vitra site,
Weil-am-Rhein,
Germany, 1994.

RIGHT
Frank O. Gehry,
Vitra Design
Museum,
Weil-am-Rhein
Germany, 1989.

THE LAW OF COMPETITIONS: A FRENCH EXAMPLE?

The situation is not new. Who knows, perhaps there was a competition to build the pyramids of Giza!

Closer to our time, in 1668, Louis XIV decided to complete the east facade of the Louvre and provide it with a face in keeping with that of a royal residence. Three men of astonishing talent, Bernini (the architect of among other things the *baldacchino* in Saint Peter's Basilica in Rome), Louis Le Vau (architect of the Institut de France in Paris and the Château de Vaux-le-Vicomte), and Claude Perrault (who built the Paris Observatory and was the brother of Charles Perrault, author of the *Mother Goose Tales*), were thus to cross swords. After the kind of politico-artistic shenanigans with which we are all too familiar today, in this battle between the baroque, the classical, and the modern, the king chose the modern, Claude Perrault.

And still nearer to us, as the 1970s dawned, the President of the French Republic, Georges Pompidou, ordered the organization of an international architectural competition for designs for a national center for art and culture to be erected on a level site in Beaubourg in the heart of Paris. Interest exceeded all expectation and entries flooded in: 186 from France and 491 from abroad. Unheard of! Chaired by Jean Prouvé, a jury boasting some of the great names in architecture, such as the American Philip Johnson and the Brazilian Oscar Niemeyer, as well as from the museum world, such as Michel Laclotte of the Louvre, Frank Francis of the British Museum, and Willem Sandberg of the Stedelijk Museum in Amsterdam, favored the plan unveiled by Renzo Piano and Richard Rogers. An Italian and an Englishman; and not a French architect in sight.

And, although he dreamed of a Greek temple, President Pompidou, to his immense and vocal disappointment, ended up with a bizarre machine. Nevertheless, he in no way called the jury's selection into question.

The competition sparked the "programmatic institutionalization" of such contests, blazing a trail not only in being the first to attract foreign architects to the French capital in their hundreds but also because the winning structure inaugurated what was to become known as the high-tech style and spawned a new approach to venues of cultural dissemination-cum-consumption.

In a nutshell, after the Centre Pompidou, nothing could ever be the same again. In 1982, President François Mitterrand launched the operation known as the "Grands Projets." In the space of fifteen years (1982–97), Paris and France in general were to see the burgeoning of a huge number of cultural spaces, some restorations and/or conversions (the Musée d'Orsay; the Grande Galerie in the Muséum National d'Histoire Naturelle; the Centre des Archives du Monde du Travail in Roubaix), others created ex nihilo (the Institut du Monde Arabe; the Parc de La Villette; the Grande Arche at La Défense; the Cité de la Musique; the Louvre Pyramid; the Bastille Opera House—all in Paris—as well as the Carré d'Art in Nîmes and the Centre National de la Bande Dessinée in Angoulême outside the capital).

A specifically French policy at the time, this explosion in competitions spawned a whole new generation of home-grown talent—such as Roland Castro, Jean Nouvel, Dominique Perrault, Christian de Portzamparc, Alain Sarfati, Francis Soler, Bernard Tschumi, and Claude Vasconi—as well as attracting a swarm of architects determined to follow in Piano and Rogers's footsteps, including Norman Foster from England, Carlos Ott from Uruguay,

ABOVE
Dominique Perrault,
Bibliothèque Nationale
de France François-
Mitterrand, Paris,
France, 1995.

RIGHT
Christian de
Portzamparc,
Conservatoire
de la Villette, Cité
de la Musique, Paris,
France, 1984–95.

FAR RIGHT
Norman Foster,
Carré d'Art, Nîmes,
France, 1993.

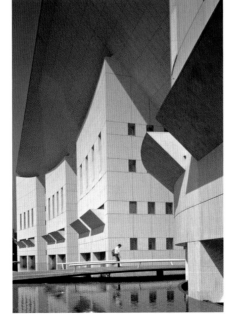

Johan Otto von Spreckelsen from Denmark, Michael Low and Richard Meier from the United States, the Chinese American, Ieoh Ming Pei, and the Italian, Massimiliano Fuksas. In short, in the space of ten years, France became the hub of international contemporary architecture. Since then, Europe and the rest of the world have made up for lost ground and there exists a profusion of international competitions, too often subjected to incomplete and/or inadequate programs. All too often the candidates and the jury feature the same names (Alsop, Foster, and Rogers for England; Calatrava and Moneo for Spain; Gehry for the United States; Nouvel, Perrault, Portzamparc, and Ricciotti for France; Koolhaas and MVRDV for Holland; Fuksas and Piano for Italy; Ando, Ban, Ito, and SANAA for Japan; Siza for Portugal; Herzog & de Meuron for Switzerland; Hadid and Tschumi when a mix of countries is called for), which might, of course, serve as a guarantee of quality and comfort, but leaves little room for newcomers.

In any case, whatever the project, a great architect or a great building cannot come into being without a great client. In general, an unbuilt project is the result of poorly expressed requirements or an ill-thought-out commission.

ARCHITECTURE, ETC.

2

ARCHITECTURE, ETC.

2

ARTISTS IN SPACE

From time immemorial, architecture has been regarded as a major art form and architects primarily as artists. The increasingly close links between architects and artists over recent years are no real innovation, but a return to the status quo after an interruption lasting a few decades. Without going back to the dawn of time, it is worth noting that before becoming architects, Brunelleschi had been a painter and a goldsmith, Bramante a painter and a sculptor, Palladio and Mansart sculptors, and Jacques I Androuet du Cerceau an engraver.

For centuries, architecture and art were closely linked: from the temple at Abu Simbel in Egypt to the Palazzo Farnese in Rome, from the cathedral of Albi, built in the thirteenth century and containing the foundations of geometric and op art in its side chapels, to the Palazzo Barberini, also in Rome, the point need not be labored. At its root, a remark by the American conceptual artist Robert Morris applies as much to the architect as to the artist: "But I want more than the object. I want a totalizing, enclosing space within which I exist with the object."

Patently, the most successful encounters arise from a confrontation between differing temperaments and idioms. Sometimes, this confrontation undergoes a transformation and, in consequence, morphs into permanence, complicity, and joint design, as in the enduring collaboration between Herzog & de Meuron and the artist Rémy Zaugg, a full-fledged member of their team. Or in that between Jean Nouvel and the light artist Yann Kersalé, who is often associated with his projects, in particular the Torre Agbar in Barcelona. Speaking of which, it is surely light that provides the most meaningful link between art and architecture. Interventions in the architectural realm by artists such as the Americans Dan Flavin and James Turrell, the Dane Olafur Eliasson, and the Frenchman François Morellet come to mind. The most intellectually thrilling experiments are indubitably those where an artist takes over a structure only to transmute it into something different, reconfiguring it and tipping it over into another dimension.

There is, however, a salient distinction between intervention and integration. In 1971, invited to take part in a group exhibition at the Guggenheim Museum in New York, Daniel Buren was excluded, due to the radical nature of his project, at the demand of the American artists spearheaded by Dan Flavin and Donald Judd. Thirty-four years later, in 2005, Buren was once again invited by the Guggenheim, but for a solo show this time—an accolade of sorts. Intervening on the object itself—the sublime architecture of Frank Lloyd Wright—he underscored the spiral slope by means of his signature alternating stripes and coated the famous skylight with colored gels, flooding the space in pink light.

The centerpiece of Buren's intervention, *Around the Corner*, deliberately runs counter to the organic curves of Wright's structure. Buren had workers specialized in building skyscrapers erect a gigantic right-angled scaffold more than 100 feet (30 meters) high in the exact center of the space and installed huge mirrors on the four faces of the construction. Since architecture and art are each the expression of a unique and autonomous creator, everything—*mise en abyme*, visual equivocation, depth and vertigo, derealization and emphasis, dialogue and confrontation—is brought to bear so that both are reciprocally enhanced, so that both resonate as one, but without laboring the point or undermining the meaning and specificities of either.

FACING PAGE

Daniel Buren, souvenir photo: Around the Corner, *of the installation,* The Eye of the Storm, *Guggenheim Museum, New York, United States 2005.*

ARCHITECTURE ON THE BIG SCREEN

It is the whole city that appears in movies, rather than "architecture." The city becomes a protagonist in its own right rather than a mere backdrop: one thinks of François Truffaut's Paris; Martin Scorcese's New York; Yasujiro Ozu's Tokyo; Roberto Rossellini's Rome (Rossellini was the son of an architect); of Berlin as filmed by Robert Siodmak (*People on Sunday*, 1930), Fritz Lang himself (*M*, 1931), Roberto Rossellini (*Germany Year Zero*, 1948), and Wim Wenders (*Wings of Desire*, 1987). One might also mention Aix-en-Provence, as lovingly recreated by Michelangelo Antonioni, or Lisbon as explored by Manoel de Oliveira. And then there's Carl Theodor Dreyer (the filmmaker responsible for *The Passion of Joan of Arc*, 1927, *Day of Wrath*, 1943, and *Gertrud*, 1964), who affirmed that, together with architecture, cinema is the most perfect form of art because neither is "an imitation of nature, but products of the human imagination."

The city and architecture are often glorified and exalted in movies, but not always. For example, the strange and disturbing *Alphaville* of Jean-Luc Godard (Golden Bear at the Berlin International Film Festival, 1965) features a bizarre scene involving doors, filmed in the corridors of the Maison de la Radio in Paris; the building, designed by the architect Henry Bernard, opened in 1963. Then there is Jacques Tati's perplexed but caustic vision in *My Uncle* (Oscar for Best Foreign Film, 1958) of a world where appearances get the upper hand and which features a futuristic house, the Villa Arpel, bristling with technological gadgets whose utility is far from obvious. Tati questions the status of the contemporary city once again in *Playtime* (1967), a chilly, timeless, dehumanized world. But, there again, Tati's analysis and questioning highlights the gulf between architecture as a creative act and the cut-and-thrust of property development that is part of the economy and of speculation; the eternal conflict of "the tree of life versus the sales spiral," as Walter Gropius (founder of the Bauhaus in 1919) put it.

ABOVE

Ridley Scott,
Blade Runner, 1982.

RIGHT

Fritz Lang,
Metropolis, 1927.

THE ARCHITECT
AS MOVIE HERO

If you haven't yet seen *The Fountainhead*, made by King Vidor in 1949, you've been missing one of the finest, most lyrical films in the whole history of cinema. *The Fountainhead* portrays an architect whose ideas are too advanced for mere mortals. But nothing can stop the film's hero, Howard Roark, in his quest, his obstinacy, or his rage. Moreover, if you haven't watched Gary Cooper in this role, you can only have a vague notion of how an actor plays a combination of elegance, determination, taciturnity, and exaltation. A movie about insubordination, *The Fountainhead* boasts virtuoso camerawork and sublime black-and-white photography where bright whites and harsh blacks interact in a subtle dialectic that is both dazzling and beguiling. Published ten years earlier, the novel *The Fountainhead* was written by Ayn Rand, a close friend of Frank Lloyd Wright, the "model" for Roark. Ayn Rand, however, refuted this legend: "[One] may be justified in seeing some parallels between Howard Roark and Frank Lloyd Wright only in a strictly architectural sense… there is no resemblance whatsoever between Roark's personal character and the character of Mr. Wright, between the events of their lives and their fundamental philosophies of life." Admittedly, Wright as a person and the character of Roark have many traits in common, but in the narrowly architectural sense one might tend to consider Roark a distant cousin of Mies van der Rohe.

Later came *The Girl in the Red Velvet Swing* by Richard Fleischer (1955), a romanticized adaptation of the murder of American architect Stanford White by a jealous husband. Then the inevitable Fritz Lang produced two fiery melodramas, *The Tiger of Bengal* (1958) and *The Indian Tomb* (1959), the story of a German architect, Harald Berger, invited by a maharaja to build a palace and a mausoleum, of his love for a dancer who has also caught the eye of the prince, and of the ensuing events.

Peter Greenaway's *The Belly of the Architect* (1987) is an entirely different film. The main character is an American architect asked to come to Rome to design and hang an exhibition devoted to Étienne-Louis Boullée, a revolutionary architect whom he admires more than any other. The exhibition was to take place in the Monument to Victor Emmanuel II, known as the "typewriter" by Romans, a masterpiece of extravagant pseudo-baroque. Things go from bad to worse and the protagonist suffers from bouts of paranoia and excruciating abdominal pains. Overwhelmed by the site and the challenge facing him, the architect goes off the rails, becomes psychosomatically ill, and can only look on helplessly as his wife becomes interested in a young Italian architect. A metaphysical reflection on complexity, on temporal and spatial presence, on the mystery and profundity of the creative act, *The Belly of the Architect*, both somber and dazzling, is a film whose idiosyncrasies are, in the end, preeminently architectural.

In 2004, Nathaniel Kahn's *My Architect*, a film which retraces the career of the director's father, the great American architect Louis Kahn, is a wholly different exercise again. This film, an exploration of Louis's four lives (his work, his "official" family, and his two other, secret families) is unexpected, unusual, and wonderfully moving. Less moving but imbued by a charming complicity between architect and scriptwriter, *Sketches of Frank Gehry*, 2005, was directed by Sydney Pollack.

Gary Cooper in the role of Howard Roark, the architect hero of The Fountainhead *by King Vidor, 1949.*

The masterly ghost of Frank Lloyd Wright has recently been summoned up once again. Author Nancy Horan has handed the film rights for her novel *Loving Frank*, regarded as an official biography, to Joel Silver, a Hollywood tycoon responsible for any number of blockbusters (producer of sagas such as *Lethal Weapon, Die Hard*, and *The Matrix*, as well as the unspeakable *Dungeons and Dragons*). The idea is less surprising than it might seem when one learns that Joel Silver is a fervent admirer of Wright and is the lucky owner of one of the famous and iconic houses designed by America's greatest architect.

LUXURY GOODS SHOWCASES

Chanel Mobile Art, born of an encounter between Karl Lagerfeld and Zaha Hadid, and promenaded with great fanfare from Hong Kong to Tokyo and New York in 2008, ended up, thanks to the financial crisis, on a terrace in Central Park. Perhaps the notion behind the Transformer, a flexible, mobile space inaugurated in Seoul in spring 2009 and designed by Rem Koolhaas for the Prada Foundation, would be able to take up where it left off. This is not Koolhaas's first dealings with Prada, as the firm is already indebted to him for several stores in the United States and he is soon to design its foundation's headquarters in Milan.

The close, even incestuous links between architecture and fashion come as little surprise. The Italian Gianfranco Ferré and the Spaniard Paco Rabanne trained as architects. As for the Frenchmen André Courrèges and Quasar (who was married to Emmanuelle Khanh, a major fashion designer who, in the 1960s, invented prêt-à-porter jointly with Michèle Rosier and Christiane Bailly, herself married to the architect Antoine Stinco), they are both graduates of one of the major French engineering schools, majoring in architecture. Then one should not forget the fascination with architecture and the cooperation with architects that affects couturiers as diverse as Issey Miyake, Yohji Yamamoto, Azzedine Alaïa, Christian Lacroix, John Galliano, and Alexander McQueen. This, too, is hardly surprising—creativity has never respected borders; moreover, clothing was the first "mechanical" environment made by humankind and is, as such, itself an "architecture" of sorts. Then there is the remarkable overlap between the languages of architecture and fashion. In short, the links are legion and almost inextricable.

In 1999, on 57th Street, in New York between Fifth Avenue and Madison, opposite the very somber IBM Tower, sprung up Manhattan's first French high-rise, built for LVMH by Christian de Portzamparc. Three hundred and sixty-seven feet (112 meters) high, it folds inward like a prism with a glass facade carved into wedges and sandblasted white so it shimmers like satin and diffracts like snow. Silk, snow, and mother-of-pearl combine to infuse Manhattan with a strangely sonorous and ultimately "jazzy" quality.

Yet it is in Tokyo, at the dawn of the twenty-first century, that the fashion-architecture partnership crystallized on a grand scale. Firstly, a Japanese quartet starting with Jun Aoki who, in 2002, designed a small glass-and-metal palace for Louis Vuitton comprising five volumes nesting like Russian dolls, hung with a lattice that is irresistibly reminiscent of the brand's celebrated checkerboard pattern. The following year, it was Kengo Kuma's turn to intervene, this time on behalf of the LVMH group, in a stylistic exercise that mixes Japanese tradition and contemporary idioms. The year 2004 did twice as well, with not only the stunningly radical six-story building by Toyo Ito, reminiscent of a tangle of branches, whose structure is lined with glass and clad in concrete, but also with a trapezoidal block that looks like it is draped in white silk for Dior designed by SANAA (Kazuyo Sejima and Ryue Nishizawa).

Secondly comes an eminently Western trio made up of the American Peter Marino who, for Chanel in 2007, came up with a monolith whose glass facade, fitted with tens of thousands of electroluminescent diodes, draws the eye to an aluminum and steel "beehive" intended to evoke the house's tweed; the Italian Renzo Piano who, in 2002, designed for Hermès a building made up of 13,000 glass blocks, as elegant and graceful by night as by day; then, in 2003, the Swiss Herzog & de Meuron erected Prada's flagship in the shape of giant diamond with five projecting lozenge-shaped translucent glass facades, some convex and some concave, and clad in concrete.

And so, from Ginza to Shibuya, from Chuo-Dori to Omote-Sando, it is in Tokyo that the marriage between architecture and fashion, between space and luxury, is truly being celebrated.

ABOVE

*Toyo Ito, Tod's Building,
Tokyo, Japan, 2004.*

RIGHT

*Christian de Portzamparc,
Dior Building, New York,
United States, 1999.*

LEFT
Jun Aoki, Louis
Vuitton Building,
Tokyo, Japan, 2004.

FACING PAGE
(on the left)
Renzo Piano, Maison
Hermès, Tokyo,
Japan, 2001.
(on the right)
Yoshinobu Ashihara,
Sony Building,
Tokyo, Japan, 1966.

3

3

forever MODERN

The First World War had finally come to an end. In 1917, in Russia, the October Revolution begat constructivism and the celebrated art schools, the Vhutemas. That same year, in Holland, the painter Piet Mondrian got together with some fellow artists and architects to found De Stijl. In 1919 in Germany, Walter Gropius established the Bauhaus, while in France Le Corbusier and the painter Amédée Ozenfant set up *L'Esprit Nouveau*.

Thus were the twentieth-century avant-gardes born and nothing, it seemed, could ever be the same again. The aftershocks of war and the decadence of art nouveau and art deco had to make way for the modern movement, for a world which had already been explored by Alvar Aalto in Finland, Adolf Loos (to whom we owe the famous "ornament is crime") in Austria, and Robert Mallet-Stevens and Auguste Perret in France.

Le Corbusier chimed in with his famous definition of architecture: "The masterly, correct, and magnificent play of volumes brought together in light." More crucially still, in 1926, together with his cousin Pierre Jeanneret, he theorized and published a vision of modern architecture called *Cinq Points d'une nouvelle architecture* (*Five Points for a New Architecture*).

First, he mentions pilotis that lift up the ground floor, turning it into a free space to allow the planting of a garden beneath the structure; then a roof terrace serves as a roof garden, a space for sport, a solarium, or even a swimming pool; the "open plan" liberates the space and allows it to breathe; long strip windows; and finally the "free facade." He was to put this theory brilliantly and convincingly into practice both in his famous white villas (the Villa Savoye, 1931) and in housing projects (the Cité Radieuse, in Marseille, 1952).

For its part the teaching of the Bauhaus (which, because of the rise of Nazism, was spread throughout the Western world, particularly in the United States) promoted minimal interiors, geometric lines, the use of new techniques, and hygienism, and affirmed that form follows function. And the pure masterpiece of rigor, simplicity, and elegance, the 1929 German Pavilion at the International Exposition in Barcelona by Mies van der Rohe, served as the flashpoint.

By 1932, at the Museum of Modern Art (MoMA), New York, the architect Philip Johnson staged the exhibition *Modern Architecture* and, with his collaborator Henry Russell Hitchcock, published a manifesto entitled *The International Style*. Both afforded pride of place to new materials such as glass, steel, and concrete, in the service of an idiom favoring smooth outer surfaces, the absence of ornamentation, wide spans, and regularity.

It was shortly after the Second World War, and primarily in New York and Chicago, that there arose the purest masterpieces of what came to be known as the International style.

Among these, the Lever Building (1952) by Gordon Bunshaft and the Seagram Building (1958) by Mies van der Rohe faced one another across a New York street.

FACING PAGE
Le Corbusier,
Villa Savoye, Poissy,
France, 1931.

RIGHT
Ludwig Mies van
der Rohe, Seagram
building, New York,
United States, 1958.

Two masterpieces
that laid the
foundations of modern
architecture and the
International style.

Even today, many architects still refer to the principles of Le Corbusier and the teachings of the Bauhaus.

Its most brilliant recent exponent is undoubtedly Enrique (later Henri) Ciriani, of Italian roots but born in Peru, who graduated in architecture in Lima and was to make his home in France. His masterpiece, the Historial de la Grande Guerre built in Péronne in 1992, is testimony to this. Built on pilotis over a lake, simple in form, with pared-down volumes and a flat roof, this structure, with its masterly deployment of light, is a paragon of modernity.

BELOW

Henri Ciriani, Historial de la Grande Guerre, Péronne, France, 1992.

FACING PAGE

Richard Meier, Douglas House, Harbor Springs, United States, 1973.

In a different register, the French architects Anne Lacaton and Jean-Philippe Vassal keep the tradition alive in their own manner, as demonstrated by the formal simplicity, vast open spaces, horizontal openings, roof terrace, long approach ramp, and flood of light that pours into their school of architecture in Nantes (2009). On the other side of the Pond, the torch is carried high by Richard Meier. His white villas, which are more than reminiscent of Le Corbusier's, prove that with more space (more land), greater (financial) means, and improved technology (techniques, materials, computation), one can steer clear of the explicit functionalism of the trailblazers and still be a part of their stylistic lineage.

POSTMODERNISM

Seldom can an adjective have been more unfortunately coined. Rather than "going beyond" modernity, what we have here is a return to the past. A tendency rather than a movement, architectural postmodernism coalesced around a book, *The Language of Post-Modern Architecture*, published in 1977 by the American architect and art historian, Charles Jencks. Postmodernism in this sense should not be confused with the "postmodernity" elaborately theorized by among others Jean-François Lyotard, who analyzes the characteristics of postindustrial societies to tease out their likely political, economic, social, and philosophical future.

Architectural postmodernism can and must be read as a reaction, in the literal sense of the word, against the modern movement and the International style.

It opts for rupture rather than continuity—but it faces backward. This rejection of what the supporters of postmodernism categorize as "puritanism" has spawned a return to ornamentation, with an accumulation of quotations, repetitions, and collages, with their content lifted from the past. To a point, it heralds the "revival" of classical or neoclassical architecture, of the Viennese Secession, of British Arts and Crafts, of German Jugendstil, of eclecticism, of the rococo, even.

Almost always verging on pastiche and tireless in its pursuit of the widest possible audience, this architecture opposes elitist and popular culture, and takes inspiration from the so-called "Beaux-Arts" tradition in, moreover, its most donnish garb. Rejecting "architecture for engineers," postmodernist architects keep one eye firmly on the "commercial vernacular" and have (literally) absorbed the astonishing *Learning from Las Vegas* by Robert Venturi, Denise Scott Brown, and Steven Izenour, to deploy the rhetoric (linguistic and visual) of advertising, while paying no more than lip service to the historical, urban, and ecological context.

The result is an anthology of caricature, the spontaneous generation of colossal "cream cakes," which can only reasonably be compared to the overblown architectural statements of the Soviet era.

FACING PAGE, TOP
Johnson-Burgee,
AT&T Building,
New York, United
States, 1984.

FACING PAGE, BOTTOM
Robert Venturi,
Gordon Wu Hall,
Princeton University,
Princeton, United
States, 1983.

ABOVE
Michael Graves,
Walt Disney
Headquarters,
Burbank, United
States, 1991.

Better than anybody
else, American
architects have
managed to avoid
the pitfalls, traps,
and vagaries of

postmodernism.
Johnson and Burgee
have done so with wit,
Venturi with distance
and erudition,
Graves with humor.

A number of architects, nonetheless, while conforming to the trend, introduce a welcome dose of humor, parody, or irony into their works.

In terms of irony, the American Philip Johnson carries the day with his AT&T Building (now the Sony Building) built in New York in 1984, seven years after the beginning of (the architectural) hostilities: a slimline skyscraper which appears to follow the strictures of the International style, but is crowned by a broken pediment knocked into a cocked hat (literally)! As to humor, the palm goes to another American, Michael Graves, with the Walt Disney Headquarters built in Burbank in 1991: a kind of Greek temple where the classical pediment is supported not on Ionic, Doric, or Corinthian columns, but by Snow White's Seven Dwarves! Turning to parody (accidental? deliberate?), the money is on the exploits of two Spanish architects, Ricardo Bofill and Mañolo Nuñez-Yanowski in the new city of Marne-la-Vallée near Paris, the first with a grandiloquent amphitheater and the second with two grandiose Camembert cheeses opposite one another.

In spite of the accumulated references and layer cake of influences, postmodernism feels like the triumph of the lowest common denominator and will probably leave little trace in history.

In 1977, then, Charles Jencks published his bible of architectural postmodernism. But the same year saw the opening of the Centre Pompidou in Paris by Richard Rogers and Renzo Piano (who was to dub postmodernism the "academism of exaggeration, surfing on waves of fashion, in the chaos of immediate gratification"), regarded by many as the eureka moment of high-tech.

RIGHT
Murphy/Jahn,
The Messeturm,
Frankfurt,
Germany, 1991.

BELOW
Mario Botta, San
Francisco Museum of
Modern Art, United
States, 1994.

FACING PAGE
Charles Moore, Piazza
d'Italia, New Orleans,
United States, 1978.

Postmodernism has
spawned many an
extravagant idea, such
as the monumental
fake obelisk by Murphy
and Jahn, the mock
mastaba by Botta,
and the pseudo-
baroque of Moore.

HIGH-TECH

Almost invariably World Fairs have played the role of accelerators—not of particles, but of experiments. In 1851, for London's Great Exhibition, Joseph Paxton erected a gigantic hall (destroyed in a fire in 1936), the glass-and-iron Crystal Palace, while in Paris, in 1889, Gustave Eiffel sent soaring over the Champ-de-Mars the metal tower that bears his name. These two architectural events are in all probability the source of what it has become customary to call high-tech architecture.

This dual influence was aided and abetted by a third, that of the Chicago School. In 1871, the capital of the Midwest was devastated by a huge fire. Once the flames died down, rebuilding started at once. A new generation of architects, with William Le Baron Jenney and Louis Sullivan at their head, started erecting a forest of skyscrapers (the elevator had recently come on the market) with reinforced steel and flat roofs. These were known as "cast-iron" buildings. This style, once confined to the factories, hangars, and warehouses born of the Industrial Revolution, was henceforth to invade the urban space. In the thirty years from 1875 to 1905 the Chicago School was to produce a flurry of technical marvels in which steel, brick, and glass go hand in hand.

As the 1970s dawned, it was in New York that the party was at its height. The southern tip of Manhattan was emptying its warehouses and workshops, thereby releasing vast spaces soon invaded by one or other of the many artistic communities that thrived in the Big Apple. **Thus was launched the vogue for lofts that was to find an echo in major cities in the Western world and in Japan, and which today is gripping China.**

At the end of the decade, in 1978, two American journalists, Joan Kron and Suzanne Slesin, brought out *High-Tech: The Industrial Style and Source Book of the Home*. A fashion was launched that soon became a trend. Kron and Slesin concentrate more on fitting out lofts and the clamorous advent of industrial furniture and objects in trendy interiors; outside things were heating up, too. The previous year, the inauguration of the Centre Pompidou had been a trigger, spawning a host of architectural outpourings, each expressing its own "authenticity."

FACING PAGE
Richard Rogers,
Lloyd's building,
London, United
Kingdom, 1984.

RIGHT
Renzo Piano and
Richard Rogers,
Centre Pompidou,
Paris, France, 1977.

To begin with,
the multicolored
piping of the Centre
Pompidou on rue
Beaubourg was
much criticized
and disputed.
Nevertheless,
it has since
been accepted.

The modernists stuck bravely to their task, however, and—vaulting or circumventing a postmodernism that to them seemed decidedly backward-looking—they started dreaming in the footsteps of Neil Armstrong, the first man on the moon in 1969. For the conquest of space became central to the imagination of the moderns—as was the everyday uptake of new technology (television, hi-fi, information technologies, multimedia, etc.), then in its infancy perhaps but clearly destined to become all-pervasive. In a manner often stigmatized as provocative, high-tech architecture glorifies the beauty of structure and proclaims its technological credentials.

Its ultimate embodiment comes in the shape of a symphony of pipes, of nuts and bolts: load-bearing, steel superstructures; external walls of glass, floating or suspended; exposed plumbing and circuitry (electricity, water, ventilation, etc.), "intelligent" flooring (equipped with multiple socketry); vertical elements of circulation (stairways, travelators, elevators, escalators) placed on the exterior surfaces—all together singing a hymn to scientific advancement. There was a corresponding fascination with the "plug-in," with the "work-in-progress" as a way of affirming that it was all experimentation, that each place was/is still in the process of becoming (progress), that new extensions can be "added on" to the construction at any time.

In a sometimes outlandish or brutal way, high-tech architecture is not afraid of exposing its "innards"—though this in no way forestalls clean-cut, "slick" objects of supreme refinement in choice of materials and treatment of light and space.

The high-tech adventure is far from over, but already its brief history boasts various icons, including, apart from Piano and Rogers's Pompidou Centre itself (1977), the Lloyd's Building in London also by Rogers (1984), the Renault factory in Boulogne-Billancourt by Claude Vasconi (1984), and the Hong Kong and Shanghai Bank headquarters in Hong Kong by Norman Foster.

Norman Foster, telecommunications tower, Barcelona, Spain, 1992.

LEFT
Claude Vasconi, Atelier 57, Métal Régie, Renault, Boulogne-Billancourt, France, 1983.

FACING PAGE
Norman Foster, headquarters of the Hong Kong and Shanghai Bank, Hong Kong, China, 1986.

MINIMALISM

BOTTOM

Ludwig Mies van der Rohe, Neue Nationalgalerie, Berlin, Germany, 1968.

FACING PAGE

Dominique Perrault, Hôtel Industriel Berlier, Paris, France, 1990.

From Mies van der Rohe's light museum structure in Berlin to Perrault's exercise in liquefaction in Paris, the objective— the obsession—is the same: the evanescence, the disappearance, the dematerialization of architecture.

The cycle speeds up, the rhythm accelerates. As in other domains, the cog wheel of architecture whizzes ever faster. The self-declared simplicity of modernism, the ragbag of postmodernity, the polemic literality of high-tech are soon succeeded by (or rather overlap with) minimalism.

It would be absurd to ignore the correspondences architectural minimalism entertains with minimal art proper, born in the United States in the 1960s in reaction as much to the subjective outpourings of abstract expressionism as to the blatant in-your-faceness of pop art. One thinks of Carl Andre for geometry or of Sol LeWitt for a sense of scale and appropriateness of the site. One again thinks of the pithy utterances of artists like Donald Judd ("No allusion, no illusion"), Frank Stella ("What you see is what you see"), and land artist Robert Morris ("My idea was not to produce an object, but to give form to space").

To give form to space: such is the ambition of those architects who embraced minimalism and tried to achieve the kind of subtle dialectical interplay that would allow the materialization of the concept to cohabit with the "dematerialization of the object," and who proclaim the idea more significant, more essential than the thing. **The result is primary, elementary structures, with clean lines, pared-down geometries, an entire paradigm based on the perception of structure and its relationship to (the) space.**

These architects were certainly not the first to express a preoccupation with extreme simplicity, with transcendent emotions. They were preceded in their quest for the absolute by the Cistercians and their monasteries and by the Shakers in nineteenth-century America. In the same way they wholeheartedly embrace Mies van der Rohe's assertion that "less is more," not forgetting that he added: "God is in the details." Engaged in a constant struggle against gravity that engages ideas of presence and absence so that their architecture adheres to, rather than obstructs, its environment, what these architects—and, therefore, the structures they build—are seeking is timelessness and asceticism. From the imagination of architects as diverse as the Frenchmen Jean Nouvel and Dominique Perrault, the Japanese Tadao Ando and SANAA, and the Swiss Herzog & de Meuron and Peter Zumthor, has sprung forth a vast array of raw, yet sumptuous buildings, wild, yet refined works which, most of the time, allow the eye to look straight through them and the mind to read them in every direction.

The minimalist architect deals in mass, configuration, density, energy, change, in dematerialization and derealization.

Their architecture may be predicated on obliteration, on evaporation, but they never abandon experiment. To the "figuration" that generally characterized the movements and tendencies that preceded and will follow them, they oppose the notion of transfiguration. Privileging once again less the form, the material manufacture of the piece, than its inner consistency as an idea: as if architecture has to preserve an element of the unfinished.

FACING PAGE

Steven Holl,
The Nelson-Atkins
Museum of Art,
Kansas City, United
States, 2007.

RIGHT

Annette Spillmann
and Harald Echsle,
Freitag Flagship
Store, Zurich,
Switzerland, 2006.

On the one side the
elegance, sobriety,
and reserve of
Steven Holl. On the
other, the economy
of means, the
temporariness,
and the humor
of Spillmann
and Echsle. Two
ways of expressing
minimalism.

NEO-BAROQUE

Baroque is not dead! In 1997—in the very teeth of the much-trumpeted victory of high-tech and minimalism—tortured, organic, biomorphic, vaguely disturbing outlines began to spring out of the Iberian soil. A structure comprised of torsion and oscillation, of crumpled metal and limestone cubes spanning disused railroad lines, suddenly came to rest on the long-deserted quayside of the Nervión in Bilbao. A bizarre excrescence, clad in hundreds of titanium plates that give it the air of a war machine, barely tamed by the gigantic dog made of plants—more kitsch than baroque—by Jeff Koons that guards its parvis. This was the year that Frank O. Gehry delivered his brand-new Guggenheim Museum.

A thunder clap, it heralded the storm to come. The following year, the Italian Renzo Piano bestowed the Centre Culturel Tjibaou upon Nouméa, New Caledonia: a building that certainly constitutes a forerunner of green, ecological, and sustainable architecture, but which, in its idiom, also looks back fondly to the baroque. Almost simultaneously, in Paris, another Italian, Massimiliano Fuksas, opened a block of residential buildings, the Îlot Candie, breaking a wave of curve and countercurve over the city in an exultant shimmering spectacle.

**So baroque is not dead.
But what is (the) baroque?**

First and foremost a feast for the eyes, a festival for all the senses that responds to mastery over space (empty and filled); to the ceaseless interplay of forms that dilate and fracture, interlock and interlace; to the supreme command of perspective; and to the delights afforded by undulation and rhythm, ellipse and exuberance, illusion and emotion, heroism and sensuality, voluptuous ecstasy and controlled ambivalence. The baroque, an art of presence, an art of the instant, of physical intensity, of the exaltation of love and death, surges forth in a paroxysm of action, in a tireless and passionate quest for beauty and joy. A rhythmic harmony that can only express itself through congruent forms that blend elegance with impertinence, rootedness with lightness, vertigo with illusion.

The sheer quantity of elements and convergences mean that here architecture and sculpture blend one into the other, without it always being possible to determine which of the two arts predominates.

Baroque is not dead, then—from Bilbao to Paris, via Nouméa, the late 1990s heralded its revival. A few years later, in 2003, the confirmation appeared in the shape of a host of buildings: in Birmingham, United Kingdom, Future Systems delivered the Selfridges department store, while in Graz, Austria, Peter Cook and Colin Fournier finished their Kunsthaus, and in Los Angeles Frank O. Gehry inaugurated the Walt Disney Concert Hall. A tidal wave of eclectic and heroic architecture.

But did this bring with it the ashlar, marble, and gold trim of baroque architecture? Not a bit: the titanium plates of the Bilbao Guggenheim, the zinc sheeting on buildings in the Candie project, the wood of Nouméa, and Birmingham's aluminum discs all testify to the fact that an architectural idiom can be adopted with its techniques and materials taking a back seat. Once again, they are but a cloak that provides the concept with a form, the idea with its material.

The metal mesh, flexible and vibratile, with which Dominique Perrault wrapped the space of the Mariinsky II project in St. Petersburg provides ample testimony. It conjures up an immense gilded shell, like a gigantic golden beetle whose carapace overflows the form of the building, engulfing but not actually touching the banks of the canal running past. Yet this gripping piece of urban scene-setting in the baroque manner still shows respect for the soul of Saint Petersburg—nicknamed "the gilded city"—so much do the shining, gleaming, dazzling constructions making up the skyline seem to vibrate in its aura.

An unbuilt project for Perrault, a completed one for Gehry, but in both cases architecture manages wonderfully to express music and dance, rhythm and gesture.

DECONSTRUCTIVISM

It was in 1968, at a time when the social sciences reigned supreme; a generation of students in architecture more politicized than their predecessors stumbled across the concept of "deconstruction" in Jacques Derrida's tome, *Of Grammatology* (originally published in Paris by Les Éditions de Minuit in 1967). Page after page, the words unfold, discontinuous, dislocated, dismantled, disjoined, disordered, dissociated—deconstructed—that is to say, in a certain manner, the negation of architecture. If Derrida strives to deconstruct Western ontology and metaphysics, perhaps it might be possible to deconstruct architecture; if not de facto, then at least intellectually, in terms of teaching, writing, or discourse?

Twenty years later, at the Museum of Modern Art in New York in 1988, the American architect Philip Johnson (who in the same space some fifty-six years earlier, in 1932, had been responsible for the groundbreaking exhibition *Modern Architecture*) unveiled a show entitled *Deconstructivist Architecture* (in collaboration with Mark Wigley). Seven architects took part: Coop Himmelb(l)au, Peter Eisenman, Frank O. Gehry, Zaha Hadid, Rem Koolhaas, Daniel Libeskind, and Bernard Tschumi, all of whom had read Derrida, as well as Heidegger, Deleuze, and Guattari, and were already showing an interest in Alain Badiou, Jacques Rancière, and Peter Sloterdijk. In short, seven architects who were theorists and ideologues, writers and readers with but few constructions to their credit. These would come later.

Still, there were projects that could already be seen to outline an architectural idiom that confronts the contradictions, dilemmas, and conflicts of the present-day head-on. These plans were accompanied by explanatory texts dripping with social science—though they were clearly subjected to other influences, in particular, in terms of form, by Russian constructivism of the 1920s, and by the "oblique function" theory devised by Claude Parent and Paul Virilio that pulls the rug out from under the feet of academic vocabularies.

The outcome was virtuoso spaces that open up: a breath of fresh air. Still on paper, certainly; but these three elements were to be found ten years later in their material realizations. If the opening salvo seems to have been fired by Massimiliano Fuksas with the slanted, disjointed facade of the Paliano gymnasium in Italy, others also favored battered walls, sloping floors and windows, off-kilter pillars that make the head spin, destabilization, fragmentation and negative polarities.

A hybrid architecture (or architectures)—often tortured, with tangential and diagonal lines, with blocks arranged in a (pseudo) random manner. Architecture that has more than one axis and vanishing point, that rejects traditional symmetry and orthogonality, that indulges in overhang and cantilever, that experiments with a host of structural devices.

Daniel Libeskind's Jewish Museum in Berlin, and Imperial War Museum North, the fire station on the Vitra site at Weil-am-Rhein, the London Aquatic Center, and the and cable-car station in Innsbruck by Zaha Hadid; and Coop Himmelb(l)au's Akron Art Museum in Ohio and Musée des Confluences in Lyon give a good picture of this architecture of controlled chaos, of apparent disharmony.

While it is obvious that minimalist and high-tech architecture are dominated by the cinematographic and sculptural, here it is safe to say that the (graphic) line comes into its own. These lines are often acute and aggressive, underscoring, highlighting a plethora of forms, an outburst of tension.

FACING PAGE

Massimiliano Fuksas, Gymnasium, Paliano, Italy, 1985.

Fuksas seems to invent deconstructivism before its time, prior to Philip Johnson's 1988 coining of the term.

Singular, solitary, "bachelor" objects, these structures don't necessarily fit seamlessly into the urban
fabric, but rely—as in every era, as at every turning
point in architectural history—on confrontation; not
on that sacrosanct integration that generally leads
to mediocrity.

In *L'Architecture contemporaine* (Scala,
2004), Sophie Flouquet quotes a short
soundbite by the Coop Himmelb(l)au which
sounds like a stab at a definition: "Our
architecture is not tame. It walks in the
urban space like a black panther through
the jungle."

shades of GREEN

RIGHT

Kengo Kuma, bamboo house nestling in the Great Wall, Beijing, China, 2008.

FACING PAGE

Jean Nouvel, musée du quai Branly, Paris, France, 2008.

Green architecture? We are only at an embryonic stage and for now efforts are concentrated more on integrating into a landscape, as Kuma does in Beijing, and on green walls and roofs, as with the glorious vertical garden designed by Patrick Blanc for the musée du quai Branly, Paris.

In November 1964 in New York's Museum of Modern Art, the architect, engineer, critic, and historian Bernard Rudofsky had organized a landmark exhibition *Architecture without Architects*, the catalog for which is today extremely hard to come by. Rudofsky focused on a number of buildings without architects over a few centuries, on vernacular architecture, both spontaneous and skillful. Though its time had not yet come, the exhibition was a revelation, an awakening. The exhibition and its catalog present a striking panorama of nomadic structures, troglodytic dwellings, houses on pilotis, and arcaded cities and villages. Including a glossary of natural and local materials (wood, bamboo, plant matter, earth, pisé, etc.), they analyze systems of natural ventilation and effects of light and shade, draw up a kind of *map* of contrivances and of making-do, of chance and necessity, focusing on ultralight dwellings in Japan (the result of its frequent earthquakes, on the cliff dwellings of the Dogon in Mali and the Hopi in New Mexico, describing underground cities in northern China that burrow through the loess and provide homes for some 10 million people. In short, it embarked on a journey without end, a voyage through a strikingly premonitory past. **At a time when the world is experiencing a serious energy crisis, when the planet is dangerously overheating, and when the population explosion brings with it a frightening increase in urban squalor, sustainability has become an urgent necessity. Our vocabulary, too, is swelling: sustainable architecture, ecological architecture, green architecture—although the exact meaning of these terms is not always clear.**

Such concern with "naturalness" is hardly novel. Already, in the nineteenth century, it had given rise to a host of "regionalist" styles, often ridiculous, petit-bourgeois pastiches of aristocratic magnificence, many of whose foibles were to resurface in the twentieth century in the epigones of postmodernism and suburban(ized) environmentalism.

Nevertheless, between regionalism and postmodernism, the modern era has spawned precursors of a worthwhile environmental architecture that manages to harness the past to progress without doing violence to either. First of all there was Frank Lloyd Wright who, in Fallingwater in Pennsylvania and the Taliesin West project in Arizona, embodied the symbiosis with nature. For the ecologically responsible side of the question, one harks back to the Finn Alvar Aalto (and his Villa Mairea); the Norwegian Sverre Fehn, nicknamed the "*genius loci*"; the Brazilian José Zanine Caldas, known as "the architect of the forest"; the Indian Balkrishna Doshi (community housing, Aranya, Indore); the Egyptian Hassan Fathy (for a novel use of unfired earth brick); the Mexican Luis Barragán with his unadulterated, colorful constructions whose ventilation owes a great deal to the traditional dwellings of the Maghreb. The list of trailblazers would not be complete without the name of Paolo Soleri, who, in 1962, set up Arcosanti, an experimental town in the middle of the Arizona desert, where he implemented his organicist arcology, a novel concentrate of architecture and ecology. And then there's the adventure of Drop City, a hippie commune set up in southern Colorado in 1965, which, although it disappeared less than ten years later, was where Steve Baer developed various formats of Richard Buckminster Fuller's geodesic domes.

Currently, ecological awareness and the need for sustainability are hot topics. Energy management (thermal, solar, wind, air, etc.), rainwater recovery, and the use of plants in and on buildings are all firmly on the agenda. The use of recyclable, reused materials and photovoltaic micro-plants is burgeoning. But has this given rise to a "style" of sustainable architecture?

In fact, there are number of styles whose starting point (confining ourselves to contemporary architecture) is surely Renzo Piano's Centre Culturel Tjibaou in Nouméa. In the heart of lush vegetation between lagoon and mangrove swamp, the architect takes inspiration from tradition but eschews pastiche, making use of all the natural sources of energy available.

This is a domain spearheaded by northern and Anglo-Saxon nations. For instance, the spruce and larch dwellings constructed by the Finn Olavi Koponen, the soil house by Martin Rauch in Schlins, Austria, the house built of straw by Sarah Wigglesworth and Jeremy Till in London, and, above all, the dwellings by the Australian Glenn Murcutt, inspired by Aboriginal thought and agricultural architecture. Japan, of course, has kept faith with its anti-earthquake tradition, even if Tadao Ando with his Museum of Water and Museum of Wood resolutely engages in a dialogue with the surrounding landscape.

For their part, in 1998, the Czech Jan Kaplický and Amanda Levete from Britain, who sign their works "Future Systems," built a house hidden away in the Welsh moors opposite the ocean, in what is a magnificent exercise in intrusion and vanishing into the scenery. Ten years later, the Frenchman Dominique Perrault, by burying the imposing Ewha Women's University in the ground of Seoul does much the same, but this time against an urban backdrop.

It is as if geography, for once, triumphs over history.

RIGHT
Tadao Ando, Museum
of Wood, Hyogo,
Japan, 1991.

BELOW
Chitra Vishwanath,
studio-house
in unfired brick,
Bangalore,
India, 2003.

BELOW RIGHT
Future Systems,
private house, Wales,
United Kingdom,
1998.

Integration, tradition,
burial: a few
ingredients of
architectural ecology.

VARIATIONS on a theme

As with any artist, writer, musician, or filmmaker, for the innovative architect there exist constants in style. Constants, that is; and not "tics," reflexes that are telltale signs of an absence of true style.

They provide a tool for extending concepts or ideas to their logical conclusion, for exploiting them thoroughly. No rehashing, no sacrificing to the trend, no flogging one specific "look"; better to give form to one's dreams, to materialize one's obsessions.

As the philosopher Michel de Certeau suggests: "The memorable is perhaps what can be dreamed of a place." And genuine architects do dream. And, because they dream, they feed the memory. Architecture is like an idée fixe. It's something that must be expressed at all costs, something that goes far beyond mere construction, mere building. How otherwise is one to "read" those recurrences, those resonances and ricochets that recur in the work of certain architects, and which, nonetheless, seem each time to harbor the promise of a new adventure, of a fresh start?

The various "radiant cities" of Le Corbusier are living proof. As are Rem Koolhaas's Del'Ava and Lemoine villas. And the Cité de la Musique in Paris and Cidade da Música in Rio de Janeiro by Christian de Portzamparc; the contemporary art museum in Barcelona and the Canal+ headquarters in Paris by Richard Meier; the Institut du Monde Arabe and the Fondation Cartier in Paris by Jean Nouvel; the Bilbao Guggenheim and the Marqués de Riscal Hotel in Alava by Frank O. Gehry; the broken lines of Daniel Libeskind's Jewish Museum in Berlin and the spirals of his Victoria & Albert Museum extension in London; the cycle track and the Olympic swimming pool in Berlin, and the Caja Mágica, the Olympic tennis center in Madrid by Dominique Perrault; Peckham Library in London and the Ontario College of Art & Design in Toronto by William Alsop; and two stadiums, the Allianz Arena in Munich and the "Bird's Nest" in Beijing by Herzog & de Meuron.

The same thing can be said of the Franco-Swiss architect Bernard Tschumi, for whom "in-between" phenomena (i.e., between space and envelope) are fundamental. Twice, in Rouen and Limoges, he won the competition for the construction of a Zénith, a concert hall dedicated to new music. In Rouen, as in Limoges, the design—without there being the least distinction between walls and roof—incorporates an envelope that encloses, from all sides, another envelope. Two sheaths, a double shell. The concrete interior envelope, identical at both venues, encompasses auditorium and stage. The outer jacket—metal in Rouen, wood in Limoges—is both rampart and form, and provides a solution to the acoustic and climatic constraints. It is between the two envelopes, in the "in-between" that people circulate, that extra-musical activities take place, that movement is distributed throughout the building. Two concert halls, then, with an identical plan, of identical size (for an audience of 7,000). In both, Tschumi follows the same spatial concept, deploys an identical architectural idiom, meets the same technical and mechanical specifications. Both are located on the outskirts of a city; but the Rouen Zénith is placed on top of a disused aerodrome which is gradually being upgraded into an industrial and commercial zone. Whereas in Limoges it is located on the edge of a luxuriant forest bordered by a vast flowery meadow. In Rouen, in what is a mineral universe, metal is king. In Limoges, against a rustic backdrop, wood reigns supreme. In both cases, two distinct voices tell the same story: the result is jaw-dropping. In the cold light of winter or under a dazzling high summer sun, the sensation is one and the same. A feeling of being confronted by solid chunks of energy, by a condensation of matter. As Samuel Beckett has put it: "Where we have both dark and light, we also have the inexplicable."

ABOVE
Bernard Tschumi,
Zénith, Rouen,
France, 2000.

RIGHT
Bernard Tschumi,
Zénith, Limoges,
France, 2007.

Two identical
accounts. Two
similar responses.
Two different
materials.
Variations
on a theme.

the CHICKEN or the EGG?

A few months apart, on the cusp of 2004 and 2005, two new towers soared into the skies over Europe. The first in London, the second in Barcelona, the former by Norman Foster, the latter by Jean Nouvel. Strikingly alike in shape, mass, and texture, both resemble *cases obus* ("hut-shells"), ribbed structures of grass and earth built by the Musgum, pony breeders living scattered between Chad and northern Cameroon. Both also irresistibly bring to mind a cinematographic reference: the rocket in Georges Méliès's *A Trip to the Moon* (1902).

The forty-one floor Swiss Re Building by Foster, known as the "Gherkin," rises 590 feet (180 meters) above the heart of the City of London. Considered to be the United Kingdom's first ecological skyscraper, its aerodynamic form means that the ventilation system is controlled by the wind, the windows being operated by a weather station. With just eighteen spaces for cars but a generous provision for cycle parking, it makes a point of its ecological credentials. A stone's throw from Richard Rogers's Lloyd's Building, the structure of the facade is treated in spirals and the thirty-eighth floor houses several privately run restaurants offering a breathtaking view over London. And at its feet, the British artist Ian Hamilton Finlay has designed an astonishing Acadian Garden.

Nouvel's Torre Agbar (Aigües de Barcelona), dubbed the "Missile," rises out of the Avenida Diagonal yards from the Plaça de les Glòries Catalanes, and measures 475 feet (145 meters) for 38 floors. Powered by solar energy and vibrating in rhythm with the equinoxes, the Torre Agbar is above all a homage to water, looking like "a fluid mass surging through a hole in the earth, a geyser whose pressure is permanent and calculated," according to the architect. Its smooth, seamless surface, quivering and transparent, underscores the aquatic allusions. The skin comprising some sixty thousand shards of translucent glass by which light artist and technician Yann Kersalé transmutes the tower into a pulsating totem pole that changes color according to the month, day, and hour. A tower of light, a tower-cum-image, which plays on the uncertain nature of matter and the perceptible.

Two towers so similar, yet so very different. Built but months apart, they were often the subject of nitpicking debates as to which is the chicken and which the egg. But such argument is pointless because awe-inspiring undertakings like these are simply impossible to modify in a few brief months. Between the decision to build, the budget analysis, the land survey, the planning development, the construction tender, the architect's vision, the technical specifications, and the development and the construction itself, years must have passed. At least four, in the best of cases. It is thus impossible to say which was "designed" first, Swiss Re or Agbar.

When ideas are in the air and the potential to realize them lies within reach, when the conditions are right and suitable techniques are available, when the zeitgeist and visual education are in agreement, it is only to be expected that different forms will enter into a dialogue, into a correspondence, and so come to express the reality of our time.

FACING PAGE, LEFT
Norman Foster, Swiss Re Tower, London, United Kingdom, 2004.

FACING PAGE, RIGHT
Jean Nouvel, Torre Agbar, Barcelona, Spain, 2005.

COLLECTIVE OR INDIVIDUAL?

4

COLLECTIVE OR INDIVIDUAL?

COLLECTIVE OR INDIVIDUAL?

COLLECTIVE HOUSING:
a challenge?

Christian de Portzamparc, The Hautes-Formes apartments, Paris, France, 1979.

In 1630, Rome, the capital of Christendom and thus of the "civilized" world, was only the fourth largest city in Italy, after Naples, Palermo, and Venice. Rome which, in spite of its pomp and circumstance, its religious and secular temples rising on all sides, was practically depopulated. So much so that participants in the races, festivals, and parades held down the Corso could see hanging from its facades vast numbers of signs emblazoned with the words: "For Rent"! Fluctuations in urban density are not new, but for two centuries the tendency has been reversed (with a phenomenal acceleration over the last twenty years), and cities are being increasingly confronted with the realities of overcrowding.

In the past, things were clear enough. The urban fabric was divided into "upper" and "lower" districts. On one side, palaces, on the other, slums. Then came Georges-Eugène Haussmann, appointed prefect of the Seine by Napoleon III in 1853, who set about reorganizing Paris according to a utopian vision that imposed order on disorder.

The order was social, certainly—in the battle against the urban diseases of squalor, lack of hygiene, epidemics, alarming death rates—but it was also political (already Paris was being transformed into a "showcase" for imperial power), economic (a surge in investment properties and speculation), and even military (the Revolutions of 1830 and 1848 were still fresh in the memory and an urban fabric of broad, rectilinear avenues makes cavalry charges and canon salvos easier in the event of rioting).

By rationalizing town planning regulations and street realignment, providing running water and improving public health, and imposing a new architectural order, Haussmann invented urbanism as we know it and the model was exported all over the world—with variations, of course.

In Berlin, Karl Friedrich Schinkel implemented a different architectural schema, taking as his starting point classical Greek architecture, in opposition to the preeminently "Roman" French taste, and defined a "rule of three" of base, cornice, and attic that remains in force today. In New York, the rationalizing spirit went in for rectilinear streets, but there the predominant factor was economic (land, rates, technical overheads, etc.), no matter the style.

France continued to innovate in the area of collective housing into the twentieth century. Shortly after World War II, while emergency rebuilding was throwing up low- and high-rise buildings.

Le Corbusier proposed a new response to the collective housing problem both in its urban and architectural dimensions. Since 1945, he had been developing the innovative and avant-garde model of the vertical garden city comprising separate ensembles inserted into the logic of a collective structure in which the individual and the group are in balance. He thus contrived an urban object, neither skyscraper nor apartment block, whose measure, ideal in Le Corbusier's eyes, is a social unit of 1,600 inhabitants divided into 337 residences of 23 different types.

For the community, there should be a nursery school, a gymnasium, a hotel, shops, and offices. The first of these housing units, built in Marseille in 1952, was baptized the Cité Radieuse. Immediately renamed the "*maison du fada*" ("house of the mad man") by the inhabitants, today it is the pride and joy of the city, and is a listed historic building. Four other housing units were to follow, in Rezé (1955), Berlin (1957), Briey (1960), and Firminy-Vert (1969). No such innovative model was to appear again before 1968.

Le Corbusier, the Cité Radieuse residences, Marseille, France, 1952.

In Ivry-sur-Seine in the suburbs of Paris, Jean Renaudie constructed a social housing project whose radicality and generosity are extraordinary: raw concrete, sharp-edged forms, vegetation cascading down from balconies in front of each dwelling, resident thoroughfares along terraces, and a variety of functions—a fresh vision of the world, of treating social housing so as to end injustice and make a "tabula rasa of the past."

Eleven years later, in 1979, in Paris, Christian de Portzamparc delivered an ensemble of dwellings he named the "Hautes Formes": a cityscape subtly fragmented into seven small buildings linked by arcades and porticos around an open passageway and a small, calm square, drenched in sunlight. A play of volume and rhythm, of line and aperture, which set up relationships and tensions that bind disparate ingredients to each other and can suddenly generate "blocks of sensation" in the urban fabric. For thirty years architects the world over have continued visiting and learning from this prime example of urban housing that lets in the daylight.

In Paris, a succession of diverse architectural idioms appeared that were equally preoccupied as much with forthright expression as with maximum functionality. There were the irregular lines and the lively reliefs of Frédéric Borel in Belleville (1983), Oberkampf (1990), and Pelleport (1999); the baroque waves of Massimiliano Fuksas in

the Candie project; the Tower Flower (2004) by Édouard François with balconies-cum-flower pots sprouting bamboo; Herzog & de Meuron's radical deployment of metal behind Montparnasse (2000); Beckmann and Thépé's building on the banks of the Seine (2008) whose concrete is so deeply, so delicately stained chocolate-brown and golden yellow that it shimmers like a bronze monument heightened in places with gold leaf. Meanwhile in Nîmes, in 1987, Jean Nouvel came up with a development of 114 apartments in the shape of a high-tech beast on pilotis. The parking lot was no longer buried underground, but laid out in the open-air beneath the building. The savings made allowed the architect to extend the surface area of what was a social housing project to that of more up-market buildings. More practically, the use of pilotis meant that the Nemausus project could avoid damage caused by the considerable spates of the River Vistre.

Worldwide, there were more and more projects aiming to bring architectural quality to public planning.

In Miami, the Arquitectonica group made imaginative use of color, bringing the sky into architecture through a gaping hole in the Atlantis Condominium (1982). In the port of Amsterdam, in 2003, the MVRDV group erected the Silodam, a ten-story building on pilotis, compacted like a tower of shipping containers from which it borrows its materials and colors, and surmounted by a teakwood terrace resembling a bridge on a boat. In 2005 in Huizen, again in the Netherlands, Neutelings Riedijk built five residential buildings literally on the water and clad in silver-plated metal sheeting that also seem about to weigh anchor. In the same year, in the charming and historic little village of Ge Inhausen in Germany, the architects Seifert and Stöckmann entirely wrapped a traditional form in a white aluminum skin without the least transition between walls and roof; 15 feet (5 meters) high, spouting out sides of the building, the living space of 237 square feet (22 square meters) on sliding rails is surprisingly transformed into a balcony-terrace.

In 2003, meanwhile, in New York's Lower East Side around round the corner from the Bowery where brick is king and the straight line the norm, Bernard Tschumi launched a shard of glass in shades of blue—hence the name, "Blue"—that juggles, twists, and overhangs in a fusion of the kinetic and the deconstructive.

It has been said that the art of the city is a thought marching through history. There will surely be further surprises in store with the astonishing urban concentration that characterizes the present century.

ABOVE

Qingyun Ma, university campus, Ningpo, Zhejiang, China, 2002.

FACING PAGE

Arquitectonica, Atlantis Condominium, Miami, United States, 1982.

FACING PAGE, TOP
MVRDV, WoZoCo, apartment building, Osdorp, The Netherlands, 1997.

FACING PAGE, BOTTOM
MVRDV, Silodam, apartment building, Amsterdam, The Netherlands, 2003.

It's one surprise after another with MVRDV, a group of Dutch architects with a caustic sense of humor: building-cum-drawer, building-cum-container, building-cum-viewpoint—imagination without end.

RIGHT
Bernard Tschumi, Blue, condominium, New York, United States, 2009.

HOUSING:
yesterday and today

BELOW

Alvar Aalto,

Villa Mairea,

Noormarkku,

Finland, 1939.

Of course, one would like to illustrate, describe, and analyze all the plans for individual housing that have marked the history of twentieth-century architecture. But one book would never be enough. It would be impossible however not to mention a number of major masterpieces, such as the Kings Road House by Rudolf Schindler in Los Angeles (1922), the Schröder House by Gerrit Rietveld in Utrecht (1924), Villa Noailles by Robert Mallet-Stevens in Hyéres (1925), Villa Stein by Le Corbusier in Vaucresson (1926), Villa Müller by Adolf Loos in Prague (1930), Casa Barragán by Luis Barragán for his own use in Mexico City (1948), or Farnsworth House by Ludwig Mies van der Rohe in Plano, Illinois (1951). At the dawn of the century, in Brussels, the Austrian Josef Hoffmann had designed Stoclet House which was completed in 1911. The idea, as the architect stated, was a "total work of art" which was to involve other artists (Gustav Klimt, Fernand Khnopff, etc.). Stoclet House was, more than just a break with the past, a harbinger, which, in the midst of the madcap forms of art nouveau, already announced cubism and art deco. Modern before its time, it continued to influence architects and designers as diverse as Mallet-Stevens, Paul Poiret, and Jacques-Émile Ruhlmann.

In 1931, the shock waves came from a glass house in Saint-Germain-des-Prés in Paris designed by Pierre Chareau for a Dr. Dalsace. The physician had purchased a private mansion at the back of a courtyard, save for the top floor which an elderly lady was unwilling to part with. No matter! Chareau hollowed out the space below the upper story and inserted a surprisingly modern house. The courtyard itself features an impressive facade constructed of glass blocks ringed by a harmonious woven metal structure, while the rear opens out onto a splendid, unexpected garden.

FACING PAGE, BOTTOM
Josef Hoffmann,
Stoclet House,
Brussels, Belgium,
1911.

ABOVE
Pierre Chareau,
Maison de Verre
(Glass House), Paris,
France, 1932.

In a short space of time, on the eve of the Second World War, in 1939, two miracles saw the light of day. Alvar Aalto devised a monument of surpassing serenity, the Villa Mairea in Noormarkku, Finland; the villa, L-shaped like many Scandinavian aristocratic residences, keeps the reception and private zones separate. In the same year, at in Mill Run, Pennsylvania, Frank Lloyd Wright finished what many regard as his masterpiece, Fallingwater House. Of unprecedented theatricality, its cubic blocks assembled in a (mock) chaotic manner, it stands immersed in dense forest, seeming to float above the all-year waterfall.

As World War II drew to a close, John Entenza, editor in chief of the sublime *Arts and Architecture* review in Los Angeles, sensing that a population boom was around the corner, launched a program of "Case Study Houses," with the goal of persuading eminent architects (Craig Ellwood, Pierre Koenig, Richard Neutra, Eero Saarinen, Raphaël Soriano, etc.) to create reproducible templates for economic and functional dwellings. Between 1945 and 1966, thirty-six models were presented, including, in 1949, one designed by Charles and Ray Eames, an example of affordability pressed into the service of an eternally youthful minimalism. It was this design that was implemented in the Eameses' private home.

ABOVE
Philip Johnson, Glass House, New Canaan, United States, 1949.

FACING PAGE
Frank Lloyd Wright, Fallingwater House, Mill Run, United States, 1939.

In 1950, it was the turn of Philip Johnson, with his Glass House in New Canaan, Connecticut, to explore exhaustively the virtues of absolute minimalism, although here there were no economic considerations. This astoundingly bright, totally transparent glass rectangle stands, like an eye-catcher, in dreamy, rolling countryside. Down the slope, a pond is flanked by a tempietto that owes nothing to modernity, while uphill an underground museum (Johnson, as director of the Museum of Modern Art's Departement of Architecture was a major collector of modern art) has been dug out of the hillside.

War, of course, often interrupts ongoing projects. In 1937, Le Corbusier had designed two semidetached houses in Neuilly for André Jaoul and his son Michel, but they were only built in 1955, in what is, for him, an unusual idiom, since the brick-and-concrete Jaoul residences (since listed as historic buildings) possess vaults and load-bearing walls. The story continued with, here and there, private houses sprouting up and providing opportunities for architects to plan, experiment, innovate, and break new ground, since increasingly and whatever the budget involved, individual commissions offered wider scope for exploration than public or speculative projects.

To each his own radicalism: Rudy Ricciotti and François Roche (R8Sie) are two major figures in contemporary French architecture, both for their standpoint and their practice; well worth keeping tabs on. In addition, confronting Vassal and Lacaton with Richard Meier is to confront two visions of the world, two economic, even political, realities, diametrically opposed to each other.

Richard Meier,
Saltzman House,
East Hampton,
United States, 1969.

Occasionally, works are born that exalt memory (Le Corbusier for Richard Meier), rigor (Rem Koolhaas), daylight (Rudy Ricciotti), lightness (Shigeru Ban), ecology (Glenn Murcutt), concealment (Future Systems), or the "non-standard" (François Roche). Meanwhile, Japan's huge conurbations, choking for lack of space and a population explosion, have spawned a special talent for inserting into the tiny creases in the urban fabric small-scale housing models that could also be true masterpieces.

LEFT
Atelier Tekuto,
Lucky Drops House,
Tokyo, Japan, 2005.

FACING PAGE
Shigeru Ban,
Curtain Wall House,
Tokyo, Japan, 1995.

5

5

CULTURE, YOU SAY?

CULTURE AGAIN
AND ALWAYS...

For centuries, the powers that be (political, financial, military, religious) have used architecture to communicate in stone. One of most symptomatic and splendid examples of the dialectic between architecture and power is surely the Villa Medici in Rome. Built in the mid-sixteenth century on the Pincio Hill by Giovanni Lippi and his son, Annibale, it presents a double face. The front facing the Eternal City is rigid, severe, unprepossessing, dark, almost brutal. This is an expression of the military, and, by the same token, political, power of Florence. "Don't mess with us," it seems to say. And yet, like Janus, the luxuriant garden front of the Villa Medici offers another face, a delicately worked, carved, rhythmical facade, frank and sunny, in what is a demonstration for Rome of its intellectual and artistic pretensions. Thus, together, the two facades come full circle, proving their point in the service of a single rhetoric.

Over recent decades, power has tended to abandon architectural gestures and objects to concentrate instead on more fluid channels such as communication, mass media, networks, and the Internet. In fluctuation, then, more than stability.

Architecture, though, has become concerned with new territories, with "communication" in all its guises whether cultural, commercial, or sporting, in keeping with the "age of leisure" and "society of the spectacle" characteristic of our time. On the cultural side, there are the three "Ms": museums, multimedia libraries, and music, with two clear trends: original design and renovation.

Museums

In the space of some thirty years, architectural creativity has flourished, with illustrations of all movements, from high-tech at the Centre Pompidou to SANAA's minimalism at the New Museum in New York, via neo-baroque at Gehry's Bilbao Guggenheim, deconstructivism at the Berlin Jewish Museum by Libeskind, and sustainability at the musée du quai Branly by Nouvel in Paris. All naturally incorporate into their plans object conservation and permanent or temporary displays, but just as much—if not more—public arenas, visitor management, and the boom in associated commercial outlets (coffee shops, restaurants, bookstores, boutiques full of spin-off products). Over time, diverse projects have enriched the museum tradition, each arriving at different planning solutions.

Thus, the multicolored museum of contemporary art of Castile and León by Mansilla and Tuñón in León, Spain, seems to resonate with the stained glass and the dazzling frescos of its almost airborne Gothic cathedral. In Madrid, a gigantic hang glider seems to extend over the Reina Sofia Museum (MNCRS) with its three buildings,

terracing, and preexisting courtyards, doubling its surface area. So buoyant is Jean Nouvel's design that it seems almost ready to fly off on a gust of African wind.

Bernard Tschumi arranged the Acropolis Museum in Athens to align perfectly with the temple overlooking it from the summit of its rock. Visitors approach the museum over a glass floor so they can peer down on to the vast field of excavation over which it is built. In MACRO, the museum of contemporary art in Rome, Odile Decq sets a strategy of hypertension against the baroque city. For the Musée Hergé in Louvain-la-Neuve, Belgium, Christian de Portzamparc composes a facade that is cut out like a panel from a comic strip.

As regards conversion and renovation, *the* masterpiece is surely that undertaken in London by Herzog & de Meuron on the power station at Bankside originally designed by Giles Gilbert Scott (who was also responsible for the famous red phone booths so typical of London), thus transforming it into Tate Modern. They turned the gigantic 115-foot-high (35-meter-high) turbine hall into a dizzying atrium, while the boiler rooms were converted into seven floors housing the exhibits, cafés, restaurants, and bookstores.

Likewise, in the German Ruhr and Belgian Wallonia, the closing of mines and steelworks created brownfield sites that needed a boost. As in Bilbao, this would be achieved through cultural outreach. The Musée du Grand-Hornu, a colossal mining complex in the Belgium region of Hainaut renovated and converted by Pierre Hebbelinck, is a prime example, as is the still more impressive Ruhr Museum in Essen, whose breathtaking spaces and volumes have been sculpted by Rem Koolhaas into elaborate itineraries for the visitor.

Rem Koolhaas, Ruhr Museum, Essen, Germany, 2006.
A magnificent example of renovation.

FACING PAGE
Luis Mansilla and
Emilio Tuñón,
Museo de Arte
Contemporáneo
de Castilla y León,
León, Spain, 2004.

ABOVE
Santiago Calatrava,
science museum,
planetarium, and
opera house, Valencia,
Spain, 2006.

LEFT
Jean-Marc Ibos and
Myrto Vitart, extension
to the Palais des
Beaux-Arts, Lille,
France, 1997.

Multimedia libraries

The same applies to multimedia libraries, which combine a multiplicity of cultural activities (exhibitions, concerts, shows, or screenings) with diverse reading practices (on paper or computer) and studios of all kinds. Often modest in size, they can nonetheless prove spectacular. In Rezé, near Nantes, Massimiliano Fuksas set up a radical confrontation between two parallelepipeds, one in light-colored smooth concrete, the other in patinated black zinc; the first straight, the other sloping, with, linking them, a glass fault line; a structure made of tension, mystery, confrontation, and seduction. The tensions are rather different in Peckham, one London's toughest neighborhoods,

RIGHT
Diller, Scofidio,
Renfro, Institute
of Contemporary
Art, Boston, United
States, 2006.

BELOW RIGHT
Patrick Bouchain,
The Lieu Unique,
Nantes, France, 1999.

ABOVE
William Alsop,
Peckham Library,
London, United
Kingdom, 1999.

FACING PAGE
Renzo Piano,
The Morgan Library,
New York, United
States, 2006.

where William Alsop has erected a library in the shape of an "L" (for Library?) standing on edge, whose flipped facade, inclined pillars, and highly diverse materials and color scheme create a strange ambience. Another bizarre entity landed in Seattle, Washington, where Rem Koolhaas built a huge angular block of a library enveloped in a gigantic net-like steel and glass skin. As for Toyo Ito, his media library in Sendai, Japan, exudes infinite fluidity and intensity, a biomorphic structure comprising an organic membrane fitted with three double-walled glass screens that morph into a magic lantern pulsating with the energy of life. Creation and rehabilitation or conversion can sometimes go well together, as in the Morgan Library, New York, where, in a design of reserve, grace, and elegance that preserves the original brownstone and the small neo-Renaissance garden, Renzo Piano has burrowed into the particularly hard ground of Manhattan and so practically doubled the surface area. As for Patrick Bouchain, he transformed the former Lu cookie factory in Nantes into the Lieu Unique, a neat, cleverly put-together multipurpose space executed with a minimum of means.

Music

In 1957, Jørn Utzon's Sydney Opera House and, in 1963, Hans Scharoun's Berlin Philharmonie provided two great new venues dedicated to music. Admittedly, the classic, proscenium theater layout is unlikely to die out just yet, but nowadays other less symmetrical, less frontal, less rational solutions are feasible. In France, in quick succession, the metal carapace of Claude Vasconi's Filature in Mulhouse and Christian de Portzamparc's Cité de la Musique in Paris sounded a different note. A series of architectural landmarks were to follow, such as the Parco della Musica in Rome by Renzo Piano, whose triple-zinc shell with spaces for three concert halls juggles resonance, assonance, and dissonance. The same goes for the opera house in Valencia and the auditorium in Tenerife, Spain, where Santiago Calatrava gives free rein to his talent for the light, the buoyant, and the evanescent in a concerto of gravity-defying forms that testifies to his mastery over both material and technique; and for the Casa da Música in Porto by Rem Koolhaas, a cubist sculpture assembled from boxes in a deceptively haphazard manner, while as night falls the accommodation ladder that serves as the entrance transforms it into a mysterious spaceship.

And then there's Jean Nouvel's concert hall in Copenhagen, inspired, according to the architect, by Scharoun, but where the wooden scales lining the auditorium seem more like a Viking longship. Without forgetting, of course, the Cidade de Música in Rio de Janeiro, recently finished by Christian de Portzamparc: two enormous horizontal planes that seem to levitate above a tangle of lagoons, mangrove swamps, and mango trees, marked by volumes devoted to the various halls in an alternation of full and empty spaces that encourages promenading and exploration, while the eye is drawn out toward the tantalizingly close Atlantic Ocean. Nor should one omit the stadium built by Rudy Ricciotti in Vitrolles, France, dedicated to new music and today left to its own devices by the original client. A radical, raw, intense, and authentic work, a charcoal gray concrete bunker plunked down in the heart of austere scenery on a rather unattractive piece of land streaked dark red with bauxite, as if washed up in the middle of nowhere.

But once again it is Herzog & de Meuron who win the prize for renovation and conversion with the Elbphilharmonie in Hamburg. Like many others, the historic Hanseatic port has seen many of its industrial activities fall by the wayside. The Kaispeicher, a one-time cocoa warehouse, an immense, disused brick-built ship conflating abstraction and realism, had long closed down. What was to be done with it? Turn it into a venue for music, housing several halls and leisure zones with restaurants and stores. Herzog & de Meuron rigged it out with an elegant set of sails built up out of crystalline shards with points soaring every which way into the sky. Towering 121 feet (37 meters) above the quayside, the Elbphilharmonie looks set to take wing above the 60 basins and 42 miles (68 kilometers) of docks, and fly off over the port, the Elbe, the Bay of Lübeck, and onto the Baltic in a perfect metaphor of a journey without end.

More modest but no less stunning is Claire Guieysse and Antoinette Robain's 2007 intervention on an administrative building built in Pantin, outside Paris, in 1972 by Jacques Kalisz, an introverted "brutalist" masterpiece, an impregnable fortress and symbol of the Communist suburbs of Paris. Intended to become a national dance center, the two architects opened the building, whose structure has been cleaned and preserved intact, onto the street and the Ourcq canal running alongside it. Hollowed out, with a hole through the entire elevation of the building, it is lit by an understated polychrome partition. Here the metaphor is choreographic, all shifting and movement.

ABOVE
Jean Nouvel,
Koncerthuset,
Copenhagen,
Denmark, 2008.

RIGHT
Christian de
Portzamparc,
Cidade da Música,
Rio de Janeiro,
Brazil, 2009.

ABOVE
Renzo Piano, Parco
della Musica, Rome,
Italy, 2002.

RIGHT
Rudy Ricciotti, stadium,
Vitrolles, France, 1994.

FACING PAGE
Massimiliano and
Doriana Fuksas, Zénith,
Strasbourg, France,
2008.

All the music
of the world, and
resonating with it,
all the architecture
of the world:
symphonic with
Piano, radical with
Ricciotti, and lyrical
with Fuksas.

FACING PAGE
Herzog 8
de Meuron,
Elbephilharmonie,
Hamburg, Germany
(to be completed
in 2011).

RIGHT
Claude Vasconi,
La Filature,
Mulhouse,
France, 1993.

Foundations by the ton

First stop Barcelona, to visit the Mies van der Rohe Foundation installed in the German Pavilion built by van der Rohe in 1929 for the International Exposition held in the Catalan capital. Dismantled in 1930, the pavilion was rebuilt in 1980 on the hill of Montjuïc and now houses the foundation that hands out the yearly Mies van der Rohe Prize awarded in conjunction with the European Commission. A masterpiece of modernism, the foundation now serves as a hotbed of European architectural research. On the very same hill, in 1975, the Catalan Josep Lluis Sert delivered the Fundació Juan Miró, whose octagonal tower, which bears a striking resemblance to a signpost, plays host to classical music concerts. Likewise by Sert, the Fondation Maeght in Saint-Paul-de-Vence, France, opened in 1964, is a pure masterpiece with a fine use of daylight and well-integrated into its environment, with sweet-smelling gardens through which sculptures by Calder, Giacometti, and Miró seem to wander at will. The Guggenheim Foundation is also active, with museums in New York (Frank Lloyd Wright) and Bilbao (Frank O. Gehry)—and soon Abu Dhabi (also built by Gehry). Another foundation, in Paris, at the Villa La Roche and the Villa Jeanneret, two "white villa" wonders built in 1923 by Le Corbusier and which have new lives as the foundation bearing his name.

For private institutions, the undisputed champion seems to be the Italian Renzo Piano. He kicked off with the Menil Collection in Houston, Texas, completed in 1987. Built to house the 16,000 works of prehistoric, modern, and contemporary art that make up the collection, it is a reserved, modest space, and yet it remains extraordinarily outgoing. As always, the control of the light is unimpeachable, the dual-function roof protecting and illuminating the art and controlling lighting density and intensity in the manner of a natural clock. Just ten years later, in 1997, close to Basel, Switzerland, Piano delivered the Fondation Beyeler, a clean, 417-foot line flanked by a park and a pond, and protected from the road by a long red porphyry wall. Inside once again the light is subservient to the artworks, a sublime collection that includes Bacon, Brancusi, Chillida, Max Ernst, Giacometti, Léger, Matisse, Mondrian, Picasso, Rodin, Stella, and Warhol. Once more in Switzerland, in 2005 Piano produced the Paul Klee Zentrum. Set in a park, its triple wave of undulating metal mirrors the surrounding hills, its light and elegant lines generating three spaces, the middle one housing the collection, while the offices, workshops, and auditorium are placed to either side. The keyword once again is integration, as the architecture and the scenery interpenetrate and enter into an endless dialogue. Spain, United States, France, the UAE, and Switzerland thus account for private foundations designed by a quintet of major architects: Ludwig Mies van der Rohe, Josep Lluis Sert, Frank O. Gehry, Le Corbusier, and Renzo Piano.

BELOW
Philippe Chiambaretta, Pinchuk Art Center, Kiev, Ukraine, 2006.

FACING PAGE
Renzo Piano, Menil Collection, Houston, United States, 1986.

But the lure of Venice remains strong; in particular for François Pinault, who, after much deliberation, has located his foundation on the banks of the Grand Canal. He started in 2006 in the Palazzo Grassi, one of the more recent and most imposing Venetian palaces, built in the eighteenth century by Giorgio Massari. Having rolled back the alterations carried out by the Italians Gae Aulenti and Antonio Foscari for Gianni Agnelli, the Japanese architect Tadao Ando set to work on the 53,820 square feet (5,000 square meters) of the palace, dividing it into forty display rooms. With lighting by the Danish artist Olafur Eliasson, in 2009 the Palazzo Grassi was joined by a new François Pinault Foundation venue, the Punta della Dogana, beyond Santa Maria della Salute where the Grand Canal meets the Giudecca Canal. Tadao Ando was employed again, transforming the historic customs house into a center for contemporary art. Preserving the essence of the sublime triangular building built by Giuseppe Benoni in 1677, he drained and waterproofed it, in addition to insulating the roof. Scrupulously respecting the traditional disposition of the warehouses as well as of the nine naves laid out laterally along the canals, Ando set a cube of his trademark smooth polished concrete that serves as a fulcrum for the whole design and contains the showrooms right in the center of the triangle and over the entire height of the edifice. The result is a work on the march of time which demonstrates that with a foundation, creation and renovation-conversion can cohabit in keeping with an era.

BELOW
Tadao Ando,
François Pinault
Foundation, Punta
della Dogana,
Venice, Italy, 2009.

FACING PAGE
Herzog & de
Meuron, Caixa
Forum, Madrid,
Spain, 2008.

Foundations set up by businesses have also become commonplace as they serve not only to enhance the firm's image, but also as a place to tie up the company's assets, more important than ever in these troubled times when economic squalls and industrial unrest lie around the corner. To create a foundation brings a business together better than scattered commissions and disparate acts of cultural outreach, though one should not gloss over the fact that advantageous ring-fencing and tax breaks (even if the situation varies from country to country) are both significant assets for larger concerns. Among such foundations, some have already reached the status of architectural icon, as is the case with Jean Nouvel's Fondation Cartier, in Paris, a buoyant and light-filled minimalist masterpiece.

The baton was then handed to Herzog & de Meuron's Caixa Forum inaugurated in 2008 in Madrid, halfway between the Prado and the Reina Sofia. In an old power station dating back to 1899, the two Swiss architects made good use of the original warm brown brick, rusting metal, and greenery. Elevating the building so that it seems to float above the urban space, each exhibition room is treated like a huge loft, the staircase undulating like a tribute to the staggering stroke of elliptical genius Borromini designed for the Palazzo Barberini in Rome. Outside, a 79-foot-high (24-meter-high) vertical garden by Patrick Blanc is one of the most beautiful stretches of plant life one could hope to see. Soon to come is the Louis Vuitton Foundation for creative art that Frank O. Gehry is planning in Paris on the edge of the Bois de Boulogne, which is to see the light of day in 2011: an immense glass box, evocative of irregularly shaped crystals, a succession of curves and breakpoints in keeping with the now Angeleno architect's style.

SPORTS STADIUMS:
a new game plan

Legend has it that, having performed his twelve labors, Hercules decided to pay homage to his father Zeus. At Olympia, the hero measured out six hundred feet (the equivalent of 192 meters), naming the distance a *stadium*, and encircled the terrain thus defined with an oval terraced bank: thus the first stadium in history was founded. As far as we know, the first Olympic Games were held in 776 BCE, and, although peaceful, they were surely just another way for Greek cities to vie against each other. Other games followed in their wake, with nearly three hundred being established throughout the Greek Empire, three of which, the Pythic, the Nemean, and the Isthmian Games, constituted, together with the Olympics, a "grand slam" of the ancient world. By the time of the Roman Empire, there existed more than five hundred, and the competitors, with due respect to legend, were veritable professionals. So much so that in 393 CE, at the behest of Ambrose, bishop of Milan, Theodosius I, the emperor of the Eastern Empire, definitively prohibited the games because of their pagan character.

Thus were the games, the laurel wreaths, and the glories all forgotten—at least until the eighteenth century, when the remains of the stadium were unearthed at Olympia. Throughout the nineteenth century, attempts to reestablish the Olympics abounded, but only came to fruition due to the doggedness of Baron Pierre de Coubertin, a Frenchman whose efforts culminated in 1896 in the first modern Olympic Games organized— as was only fitting—in their birthplace, Athens. In 1900, in tribute to Coubertin, the second games were held in Paris.

As time progressed, competition between rival countries to stage the Olympic Games gained pace considerably, first to gain political advantage, then, increasingly, for economic and PR reasons, as well as to boost tourism. Today, the Olympic Games are broadcast on television and over the Internet to a billion viewers, providing an occasion, once again, to put a country's sporting prowess to the test in a suitable architectural showcase.

This was already true in 1972, with the tensile structures erected over the Olympic Stadium in Munich, and again in 1976, in the Montreal Olympic complex built by Roger Taillibert. Yet, for an Olympic venue conceived in terms of image as much as in those of structure, the peak was undoubtedly reached in 2008, with the Olympic Stadium in Beijing. So evocative was the form given to it by the Swiss Herzog 8 de Meuron that this complex arrangement of lines was nicknamed the "Bird's Nest." This was joined by the National Aquatics Center, dubbed the "Water Cube," as it, too, was endowed with an eloquent form and texture by PTW Architects (in association with the engineering firm Arup). Both these constructions are even more magnificent at night, when they metamorphose into gigantic urban glowworms.

On one hand are the challenges integral to a new type of stadium that has to be designed as a commercial hub as well as a sporting venue; on the other, there is the need for architectural flair in keeping with the Olympic spirit: the result is multipurpose venues that almost immediately obtain iconic status.

Following the example of the Olympic swimming pool and cycle track in Berlin and the Olympic tennis center (already dubbed the "Magic Box") in Madrid, both by Dominique Perrault, and which vacillate between minimalism and high-tech: the Allianz Arena, the soccer stadium in Munich, again by Herzog 8 de Meuron, of which the same might be said; the archery arena designed by Enric Miralles for the 1992 Olympic Games in Barcelona; Zaha Hadid's astonishing and highly "deconstructivist" ski jump in Innsbruck; the very modernist, snow-white Charléty Stadium in Paris, designed by the father-and-son team of Gaudin; and the planned sustainability of the Guadalajara soccer stadium by Jean-Marie Massaud and Daniel Prouzet that is, more than a "cauldron," a crater dug into the heart of an artificial green hill that dominates the landscape: Volcano Stadium is expressive of the conjunction between the energy of the earth and that of sporting endeavor.

ABOVE

Herzog & de Meuron,
The Bird's Nest,
the Beijing Olympic
Stadium, China, 2008.

RIGHT

Herzog & de Meuron,
Allianz Arena, Munich,
Germany, 2005.

BELOW

Chaix and Morel,
La Licorne Stadium,
Amiens, France,
1999.

ABOVE
Dominique Perrault,
velodrome and
Olympic-size
swimming-pool,
Berlin, Germany,
1999.

BELOW
Eduardo Souto de
Moura, municipal
stadium, Braga,
Portugal, 2004.

ABOVE
Jean-Marie
Massaud,
Volcano Stadium,
Guadalajara,
Mexico, 2009.

FACING PAGE
CSCEC + PTW +
CCDI and Arup,
National Aquatics
Center, Beijing,
China, 2008.

public places?
common spaces?

Nowhere else are architects confronted by the representation of power and by the expression of symbols (of whatever nature) to the extent they are in public places: at least in their everyday guise, as buildings for government, justice, education, health and safety, transportation, or infrastructure. It is also here that the general population comes face to face with the architectural discourse of an institution which nowadays often explicitly takes on contemporary values such as transparency, efficacity, modernity, and conviviality—even if there remains a hint of grandiloquence, or the architect brings a glimmer of antagonism or radical opaqueness to his work.

Jean-Marc Ibos
and Myrto Vitart,
fire station,
Nanterre,
France, 2004.

It is hard not contrast the monumentality of Tokyo's City Hall by Kenzo Tange with the buoyant dome of Norman Foster's Reichstag. Similarly it seems obvious that France, with a veritable slew of law courts (Richard Rogers in Bordeaux, Christian de Portzamparc in Grasse, Claude Vasconi in Grenoble, Jourda and Perraudin in Melun, and Jean Nouvel in Nantes), appears to be showing off. And what a yawning chasm between the highly "urban" high school built by Jacques Hondelatte in Bordeaux and the "bucolic" aura of Duncan Lewis's in Fredrikstad, Norway; and between the shaded Le Fresnoy art center by Bernard Tschumi and the light-drenched school of architecture in Nantes by Lacaton and Vassal or Christian Hauvette's ecological education authority building in Fort-de-France. Similarly, there is a stark contrast between the daylight flooding into the Maison de Solène by Ibos and Vitart and the artificial illumination of the thermal baths at Dax by Jean Nouvel. In short, idioms, styles, and intentions overlap, interconnect, and enter into dialogue in this area as they do elsewhere, often in response to wholesale shifts in practices, amenities, and specifications.

In 1974, with the compact, self-contained airport at Roissy 1, Paul Andreu invented, if not a new style of air travel, at least a novel and effective way of managing passenger flow. The exponential growth and acceleration in airline customer numbers has since upped the ante. Airports have become linear, sometimes stretching for miles, and have been the stage for some architectural masterstrokes, such as Norman Foster's in Beijing, Richard Rogers's in Barajas (Madrid), and Renzo Piano's in Osaka. Rail transport has not escaped these developments and stations, too, are changing. The example of the French high-speed train, the TGV, and its exportation have turned the limelight on models for stations by the French architect Jean-Marie Duthilleul.

LEFT
Frédéric Borel,
architecture school,
Paris, France, 2008.

BELOW
Duncan Lewis and
Pir II Arkitektkontor,
AS, experimental
junior high school,
Fredrikstadt,
Norway, 2003.

Then there is infrastructure—especially viaducts, bridges, and walkways—a time-honored focus for architectural daring. Projects range from the modest, such as the footbridge thrown over the Areuse in Switzerland by Geninasca and Delefortrie, to the most spectacular, like the viaduct at Millau, France, strung across the abyss by Norman Foster, via the technical tours de force of Santiago Calatrava, in particular in Buenos Aires, and the visual flexibility and extreme user-friendliness of the Simone-de-Beauvoir footbridge in Paris by Dietmar Feichtinger, with, as a final flourish, the footbridge over the River Mur in Graz, Austria, by the artist Vito Acconci—artwork, walkway, café, and theater.

FACING PAGE, TOP
Norman Foster,
Reichstag Dome,
Berlin, Germany,
1999.

FACING PAGE, BOTTOM
Odile Decq and
Benoît Cornette,
viaduct and A14
highway control
center, Nanterre,
France, 1996.

RIGHT
Kenzo Tange, City
Hall, Tokyo, Japan,
1991.

LEFT
Jean-Marie
Duthilleul, TGV
Station, Avignon,
France, 2001.

FACING PAGE
Norman Foster,
airport, Beijing,
China, 2008.

LEFT
Otto Steidle,
Ulm University
West Campus,
Germany, 1994.

FACING PAGE
Dietmar Feichtinger,
Simone-de-Beauvoir
footbridge, Paris,
France, 2006.

public places,
private places

In 1977, John Portman delivered in rapid succession the Bonaventure Hotel in Los Angeles and the Renaissance Center in Detroit, thus inaugurating his famous atriums which were to virtually revolutionize the hotel business, and which he was to reuse at the Hyatt Regency Atlanta and San Francisco, and the Mariott Marquis New York and Atlanta. The basic idea is a tower hotel with a central void stretching the entire height ringed by walkways instead of corridors and, most importantly, with glass-fronted elevators looking down into the abyss gliding up and down in an endless ballet. Lambasted for showmanship and lavishness (the word "bling" wasn't yet coined), Portman nevertheless kicked off a trend that propelled the "grand hotel" into the modern age.

LEFT
Jean Nouvel,
Saint-James Hotel,
Bouliac, France,
1989.
FACING PAGE
John Portman,
Mariott Marquis
Hotel, Atlanta, United
States, 1985.

The second stage in the ascendency of purple and fine linen we owe to Philippe Starck with his Royalton (1988) and Paramount (1990) hotels, both in New York. These were followed by the St Martin's Lane and the Sanderson in London, and then the incredible Delano in Miami. And what links Portman and Starck? A taste for the elaborate and a nose for location, their sense that the public they address is more concerned with seeing and being seen than with the kind of delicious tête-à-têtes for which old-style deluxe hotels, such as the Pierre in New York, the Plaza Athénée in Paris, Raffles in Singapore, the Rambagh Palace in Jaipur, or the Peninsula in Hong Kong were intended. So much for venerable and international luxury hotels. There have also sprung up what have become known as "boutique hotels," which have mushroomed over recent decades in designs by talents as diverse as Andrée Putman (the Morgans in New York and Im Wasserturm in Cologne), Frank O. Gehry (the Marqués de Riscal in Elciego), and Jean Nouvel (the Saint-James in Bouliac). Nevertheless, and in spite of the trend for bijou city-center hotels where the comfort, design, and decor are only equaled by the service and discretion, "architectural carbuncles" continue to bloom, as in the Atlantis Hotel, Dubai, produced by the American firm, SOM, whose frighteningly overblown inauguration remains etched in the memory.

ABOVE
Skidmore, Owens, Merril, Atlantis Hotel, Dubai, UAE, 2009.

FACING PAGE
Frank O. Gehry, Hotel Marqués de Riscal, Elciego, Spain, 2009.

Here, the overblown is visible both in the "too much" of Dubai and in the expressiveness of Elciego.

heaven on earth

To enter the basilica of Sainte-Marie-Magdalene in Vézelay, the cathedral of Santa Maria Assunta in Torcello, the temple of Abu Simbel in Egypt, the Süleymaniye Mosque in Istanbul, and so many other churches, chapels, temples, mosques, and synagogues, leaves even the atheist feeling irrepressibly uplifted. It is as if places of worship constitute a kind of architectural perfection. Veritable "books of stone," in which faith, symbolism, meaning, hagiography, history, and culture coalesce—not forgetting a sense of power and glory that is no longer virtual and immanent but tangible and quantifiable. Among so many examples, one in particular springs to mind: the baptistery of the cathedral of Santa Maria dei Fiore in Florence, whose sublime doors carved by Lorenzo Ghiberti evoke both the entry into paradise and the inexhaustible splendor of the Church. Architects still quench their thirst at this flowing spring—if with varying degrees of success.

The much-vaunted chapel of Las Capuchinas, built in 1960 in Mexico by Luis Barragán, provides a wonderful illustration of the architect's own dictum: "Only through infinite communion with solitude can man find himself." And it is indeed by being reserved that architecture best expresses itself in this field. Many architects, such as Ando with the Komyo-ji Temple in Ehime, Japan; Le Corbusier with Notre-Dame-du-Haut in Ronchamp, France; Sanaksenaho with the Saint Henry's Ecumenical Art Chapel in Turku, Finland; Zumthor with the Bruder Klaus Field Chapel in Wachendorf, Germany; Wandel, Hoefer, Lorch with the Ohel Jakob Synagogue in Munich, Germany; and Parent and Virilio with Sainte-Bernadette-du-Banlay in Nevers, France, have confronted the question with talent and humility. But perhaps none quite outdoes Tadao Ando with his Church of Light in Osaka: the epitome of simplicity, elegance, and meaning. The perfection of nothingness.

FACING PAGE
Luis Barragán,
convent and chapel
of Las Capuchinas
Sacramentarias
del Purisimo
Corazón de Maria,
Tlalpan, Mexico,
1953–60.

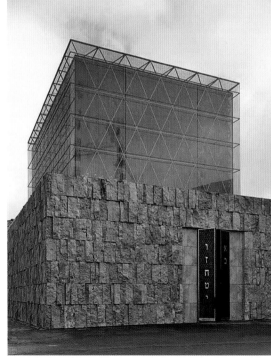

TOP
Toyo Ito,
Crematorium,
Kakamigahara,
Japan, 2006.

LEFT
Wandel, Hoefer,
Lorch, Ohel Jakob
Synagogue, Munich,
Germany, 2006.

ABOVE
Vedat Dalokay,
King Faysal
Mosque, Islamabad,
Pakistan, 1986.

FACING PAGE
Sanaksenaho, Saint
Henry's Ecumenical
Art Chapel, Turku,
Finland, 2005.

DREAM MACHINES

UTOPIA: order or disorder?

"Utopia is simply something that hasn't been tried yet," affirmed naturalist and explorer Théodore Monod, who had crossed many a desert in which he would have easily felt in the middle of nowhere. And in point of fact the word *utopia* literally means "nowhere," a "place that does not exist."

In the sixteenth century, the English writer and philosopher Thomas More dreamed of his island of Utopia as home to an ideal society in which human society is regulated by mechanics or harmony.

This dream is relatively close to that outlined by Plato in *The Republic*, and later Henri de Saint-Simon, Charles Fourier, George Orwell, and Ernst Bloch. Pushed to the extreme, utopian ideals lead to totalitarian doctrines, whereas in current usage the word has become synonymous with an unrealizable dream, an irrational, over-intellectualized construct, rehearsing the time-worn debate between order and disorder, organization and the organic, ideology and ideal, dream and reality.

In the realm of architecture, this opposition is no less enduring and the two adversaries have always had to cohabit, from the archetypal labyrinth to the Tower of Babel, the ideal city, French Revolutionary architecture (Boullée, Ledoux, Lequeu), the garden city, and the Cité Radieuse of Le Corbusier, down to Parent and Virilio's "oblique function."

"The utopian thinker looks on human life and society as a term in an equation. He only analyzes the perfect, timeless and anonymous world of numbers so as to make man a timeless, anonymous, and perfect object. He elucidates the cosmic system, not to ensure man's sovereignty over it, but to turn man into a system ... He forces anomalies to conform to the norms of a plan. He organizes the unpredictable into monotony, disorder into regularity, chance into logic. He pours our desires into the unyielding mold of necessity and would prefer freedom to wither and die as long as that equality triumphs ... He is fanatical about structure. His dream: to inject structure into human life, into societies and peoples generally," writes Gilles Lapouge in his *Utopie et Civilisations* (Weber, 1973). And Lapouge continues: "The counter-utopian is a man of passion. His specialty is not reality, but the desirable ... He turns his back on logic, proud to snub common sense and reason. The man of history is a dialectician. He is less interested in designing structures than in interactions between events along the line of becoming. He is a man of metamorphosis. Whereas the utopian is completely devoid of a sense of dialectic. Of what use would it be to him? He 'hates the movement that shifts the lines.' He is a logician." In short, the question remains unresolved: is utopia order or disorder? And is the utopist a dreamer or a realist?

In this respect, it is both interesting and amusing to note that in the fifth century BCE a single man, Hippodamus, was the original architect and utopist, described a century later by Aristotle as "he who invented the geometrical layout of cities." He was given the responsibility of rebuilding the town of Miletus leveled by war. Thus he came up with a new urban model; the city as chessboard, the orthogonal city, composed of identical streets laid out at right angles.

*Archizoom Associati,
Wind Town, utopian
project, 1969.*

From this utopian idea of the city and of the buildings it contains came the best and the worst, from country houses to new towns, from monasteries to concentration camps, from Beijing to New York and from Chandigarh to Brasilia, from the Instant City (devised in the 1970s as an exercise in liberation by the Florentine group Archizoom) to the Parc de La Villette, Paris, designed on a rigorous lattice of lines and points by Bernard Tschumi.

contemporary UTOPIAS

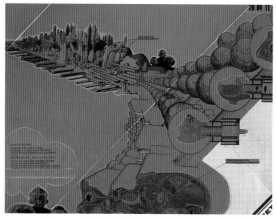

"Those were happy days; pity no one told us they were," notes Frédéric H. Fajardie in *Chronique d'une liquidation politique* (La Table Ronde, 1992).

Emerging from the Second World War and on the threshold of the postwar boom, groups of young architects, determined to reinvent the city, architecture, and life itself, started coalescing. They didn't really have masters, but "inspirers": Richard Buckminster Fuller, for one, architect, inventor, designer, and writer, chased out of Harvard for "lack of ambition," a true genius, whose geodesic domes filled their dreams; and Yona Friedman, whose projects for "space cities," megalopolis-continents above the ground forming endless urban ribbons, filled them with wonder; and Cedric Price, with his fat cigars and boundless joie de vivre, whose plans for a Fun Palace in London and an itinerant university housed in railroad cars running on abandoned track delighted them.

Such fascination, amazement, and enchantment led to concepts of flexibility, lightness, mobility, and nomadism. With, as their credo, a short saying of Cedric Price's: "Technology is the answer, but what was the question?"

And what did all these groups have in common? The will to do battle, a political (but non-party political) conscience, a desire to roll back the frontiers, and a toolbox containing desire, delight, humor, irony, imagination, and talent.

In London, in 1961, Peter Cook, David Greene, Ron Herron, Warren Chalk, Dennis Crompton, and Michael Webb founded Archigram, publishing—since they couldn't build them—projects influenced by pop art, comic strips, space research, and the fledgling phenomenon of mass media. Accumulation and profusion were the constants in these playful, poetic, and provocative projects. They prefigure what came to be called high-tech, preempting and denouncing a society based on the transitory, the consumable, and the throwaway.

In 1966, in the heart of the Florence architecture faculty, Andrea Branzi, Gilberto Corretti, Paolo Deganello, Massimo Morozzi, and Dario and Lucia Bartolini set up the collective Archizoom, while Adolfo Natalini and Cristiano Toraldo di Francia founded the group Superstudio. Through complicity, emulation, and rivalry these two groups turned Tuscany into a hotbed of the utopian imagination, of the unrealizable dream. From instant cities to Radical Design, they forged a storehouse of ideas and a formal vocabulary that still prevails. In 1968—while, from Paris to Mexico City, from Rome to Los Angeles, from London to Tokyo, the festival of love was at its height—the backwoods of Texas saw the birth of the Ant Farm group, founded by Chip Lord, Hudson Marquez, and Doug Michels. Less architects than conceptual artists, they employed the new-fangled technology of video to broadcast their manifestos. Their most groundbreaking realized project was the amazing Cadillac Ranch, built in 1974 in Amarillo, Texas, by the roadside of Interstate 40.

It looked like what it was: a row of ten used Cadillacs dating from 1949 to 1963 stuck in the ground at an angle equal to that of the sides of the Great Pyramid of Giza. A vibrant homage to architecture without architects, to land art and to arte povera, as well as a resounding challenge to an ever more invasive consumer society. In 1967 and 1968, in Vienna, Austria, two groups arose: Haus-Rucker-Co (Laurids Ortner, Klaus Pinter, and Günter Zamp Kelp) and Coop Himmelb(l)au (Michael Holzer, Wolf D. Prix, and Helmut Swiczinsky), the former earning notoriety for its physical experiments and for the development of some bizarre contraptions, such as the Mind Expander, an inflatable love couch for two fitted with a headset allowing the wearers to attain a state of ecstasy by means of electrotactile stimuli, and for the Riesenbillard, a blow-up environment for a hundred people. In Vienna, as in London, Florence, Amarillo, and elsewhere, both groups were intent on experimenting, on planning, on peering into the future, on keeping one step ahead.

But they all proved to be a flash in the pan. By the end of the 1970s all these agitators and producers of striking ideas and images were to become extinct—Coop Himmelb(l)au excepted, which reappeared under the same name and became associated with deconstructivism, continuing to engage in a compelling architectural practice—though certain individuals, such as Peter Cook and Ron Herron, Andrea Branzi, and Paolo Deganello, are still talked about today. The dream is over, but the memory lives on, vivid and vibrant.

FACING PAGE
Haus-Rucker-Co,
Leisuretime Explosion,
c. 1965.

BELOW
Archigram/Peter Cook
Instant City, utopian
project, 1993.

real UTOPIAS?

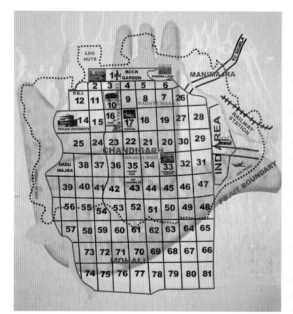

Is the ideal city, an architecture of liberation, even conceivable? Many attempts have entered the annals of history (including two recent examples that remain controversial), some rejecting, some accepting ideology and ideal, between dream and reality: Chandigarh in India and Brasilia in Brazil.

Le Corbusier,
Plan for Chandigarh,
India, 1951.

In 1951, four years after the independence of India and the violent and destructive War of Partition with Pakistan, Pandit Nehru employed Le Corbusier for the task of designing a new capital. Punjab was amputated during Partition and its one-time capital, Lahore, now found itself in Pakistan.

With the assistance of Edwin Fry, Le Corbusier imagined and planned the new city of Chandigarh following a preeminently utopian schema: sixty squares with numbered sectors (but without a number 13, since the architect was superstitious) with sides 1 mile (1.5 km) in length. Built in accordance with the ancient wisdom of the local vernacular architecture, Chandigarh already hints at a concern with ecology, with its roof-terraces, sun-blinds, and windows oriented in accordance with the prevailing winds to aid air circulation. In what was an orthogonal city laid down with a ruler, Le Corbusier nevertheless circumvented his theory of the straight line (The curve is the "pack-donkey's way" he was heard to say), introducing here or there bends and waves that prefigure Notre-Dame-du-Haut, the church he planned at Ronchamp (1955). Built in less than a decade (1952–59), Chandigarh boasts the greatest concentration of Le Corbusier's architecture on earth: the governor's palace, the legislative assembly, the law courts, the museum and art gallery, the art school, the sailing club, and, a minor marvel of sobriety, the Villa Sarabhai.

Conceived in the modern image of India and as the capital of Punjab, planned to house some 150,000 inhabitants, Chandigarh today contains more than 600,000. Moreover, as the original Punjab has since been split into the three separate states of Punjab, Haryana, and Himachal Pradesh, Chandigarh, located on the borders of all three, belongs to none in particular, a fact

Le Corbusier,
Legislative Assembly,
Chandigarh, India,
1955.

Le Corbusier,
Villa Sarabhai,
Chandigarh, India,
1953.

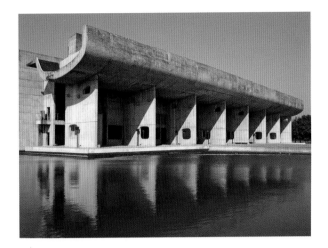

that no doubt partly explains its current poor state of conservation.

The idea was rather different in Brazil. Elected president of the republic in 1956, Juscelino Kubitschek decided to endow his federal state with a new capital: Brasilia, located in the Central-West Region at the heart of the country. Lucio Costa organized his development plan of rigorous and orthogonal sequences of generic form into the shape of a bird with outspread wings (oddly reminiscent of some of the mysterious geoglyphs observed in Nazca, in nearby Peru), set within a gigantic artificial lake whose two main axes seen from above look like a fuselage with wings. Kubitschek and Costa dreamed on a grand scale, with 2,500,000 inhabitants living in "a model city, beautiful and monumental."

If Lúcio Costa was concerned with overall planning, Oscar Niemeyer, the poet of concrete, turned his hand to the architecture. Within the severe core of Brasilia he placed an unparalleled modern tropical baroque, the acme of which is attained in the Presidential Palace, the National Congress, the Supreme Court, the Ministry for Foreign Affairs, and, especially, in the

Cathedral of Nossa Senhora Aparecida. Inaugurated on April 21, 1960, by President Kubitschek, hardly a thousand days after the first pickaxe came down, Brasilia is a surprising blend of rigorous, ordered utopia and lyrical, joyous counter-utopia.

Few architects have produced projects of such scope since. Brasilia and Chandigarh are both moreover wonderful illustrations of the conflict between order and disorder that still feeds the utopian debate. Yet, in the end, in India as in Brazil, it was not regularity and organization that had the last word, but disorder and organicism, as testified by the wrinkles, cracks, holes, and fractures that pepper Chandigarh, and the teeming life on the outskirts of that monument of perfection, Brasilia. In what direction do we go, then: from dream to reality—or from reality to dream?

ABOVE
Oscar Niemeyer,
cathedral, Brasilia,
Brazil, 1970.

ABOVE RIGHT
Oscar Niemeyer,
Presidential Palace,
Brasilia, Brazil, 1960.

FACING PAGE
Oscar Niemeyer,
National Congress,
Brasilia, Brazil, 1960.

AND WHAT WILL TOMORROW BRING?

It is still far too early to say for sure, but we can already spot architects and trends on the horizon that are likely to become the benchmarks of the future. The buzzwords? Radicalism, ecology, lightness, irregularity, experimentation.

Poets and writers testify that change is and always has been the same: an eternal new beginning, not a series of rifts and fresh starts, but a question of pushing boundaries.

As Goethe said: "to remain immobile means to submit." Architecture, as with art, literature, music, and cinema, is only worthwhile when it explores new territories, coins new languages, and imagines new symbols and meanings. All around the world, in China, Japan, Spain, Italy, the United States, the United Kingdom, France, and the Netherlands, the talents that will devise the architectural landscapes of tomorrow are emerging or asserting themselves.

Japan's dearth of land and burgeoning population have led to some exemplary efforts at "miniaturization." Japanese architects have become masters of the small form, in building dwellings that can be dropped into the tiny gaps in the country's tightly woven urban fabric. This is the case with, among many others, Atelier Bow-Wow (Mini House), with Shuhei Endo (Rooftecture), with Masaki Endoh (Natural Ellipse), and with Terunobu Fujimori (Nira House).

In China, the demands are different since the "Middle Kingdom" is currently confronted with the kinds of urgent problems and essential needs that Western European nations faced shortly after the Second World War. Nevertheless, in the tidal wave of construction presently engulfing China, a few nuggets do emerge, such as Qingyun Ma, a one-time associate of Rem Koolhaas, whose Village Hotel in the Jade Valley is an example of tradition reinterpreted; Gary Chang, whose Suitcase House, one of nine composing the "Commune" village lodged in the Great Wall, is an ingenious and elegant joy; MAD Studio's tower outside Toronto presently under construction is highly "Zahahadidian" in inspiration. These are exemplary of what Frédéric Migayrou, head curator of architecture at the Musée National d'Art Moderne-Centre Pompidou, has described as "non-standard" architecture, as is the American agency Asymptote's Hydra Pier built between earth and water on a polder in Haarlemermeer in The Netherlands, which resembles a surfboard about to take off. In the same "non-standard" register, the Erasmus Bridge in Rotterdam and the Mercedes-Benz Museum in Stuttgart, by the Dutch group UNStudio are, already, in their different ways, indications of the future.

FACING PAGE, TOP

Studio Arne Quinze, Uchronia, Message out of the Future, Burning Man Festival, Black Rock City, United States.

FACING PAGE, BOTTOM

Álvaro Siza Adega Mayor, Campo Maior, Portugal, 2006.

With their temporary timber structure burned at the end of the festival, the architects demonstrate how computer-aided design makes every calculation, and therefore every form, feasible.

In this minimalist winery lost in the midst of the vineyards, a work by the greatest Portuguese architect, yesterday, today, and tomorrow meet in clean lines that stretch out beneath the infinite sky.

DREAM MACHINES

In a more ecological vein, one finds the Frenchman, Édouard François, and the Scot (based in Bordeaux) Duncan Lewis; or else, Andrés Jaque from Madrid, whose Bubble homes have made a lasting impression, as well as the group Ecosistema Urbano, also in the Spanish capital, whose Ecoboulevard, an ecologically minded public space currently being laid out on the periphery of Madrid, promises to be pretty adventurous. More traditional, the RCR group of Barcelona is putting the final touches to the Musée Soulages in Rodez, while their Bodega Belloc on the hill above Barcelona, and Les Cols restaurant in Olot, five blocks made of glass apparently floating in the landscape, are especially welcome.

Others harbor still more radical notions, such as Italy's Group 5+, the BIG group in Denmark, and the French duo of Combarel and Marrec, whose fluid Centre RATP in Thiais, battered deep into the ground, is exemplary; others meanwhile continue to flirt with art proper, for instance the Franco-Portuguese Didier Faustino with his Bureau des Mésarchitectures or Adjaye, whose British Pavilion at the Venice Biennale, produced in conjunction with the Danish artist Olafur Eliasson, remains etched in the memory.

More experimental, the Belgian Julien De Smet (qualified, like so many others, as a "boy Koolhaas"), a conceptual architect whose public space in the port of Copenhagen (with assistance from Bjarke Ingels) affords a splendid illustration of the "almost nothing" (*le presque rien*) dear to philosopher Vladimir Jankélévitch; another *presque rien* is conjured up by the architects of the NL group (more "Koolhaas boys"), with their Basket Bar in the University of Utrecht that combines a basketball court and a bar in near weightlessness; no less venturesome, the Media-TIC building in Barcelona, of stretched metal and textile, on the outskirts of the Catalan city, in the heart of a district dubbed "B@22," is another tour de force.

No less fabulous is the astonishing art gallery in Tokamashi, Japan, by the French R&Sie (an abbreviation of François Roche and Stéphanie Lavaux, pronounced "*hérésie*"), whose output is, if outstanding, relatively restricted—though François Roche, who teaches at the Columbia University, New York, a much-traveled lecturer with a welter of publications, exhibitions, as well as outbursts, to his name, is considered in the eyes of a number of young architects and students as an intellectual guru: a parking lot apron borne on slanting pilotis that can be elevated to expose a staggering exhibition space, whose effectiveness is only equaled by its wit.

In short, from every point on the compass, all the ingredients are already in place to be made, in ten years time, into another book no less full of surprises than the present volume.

The IT revolution has also proved a formidable boost to creativity. Now everything is possible and utopia seems a thing of the past. As for the avant-gardes, the underground, and new dawns, the explosion of the Internet represents a triumph: nothing can pass unnoticed today. Any idea, any concept, any project can be found instantly on Google or Twitter.

ONWARD AND UPWARD

8

THE CURSE OF BABEL

"In the beginning was the Word," Genesis tells us. To which the poet Louis Aragon retorted: "The word was not given to man, he had to take it!" In all events, the intersecting history of architecture and language, of the tower and the unification—or the confusion—of languages is eternal.

A long time ago, a very long time ago, in Babylon, at a time when all those who had escaped the Flood in the Ark spoke the same language, the sons of Noah started building the Tower of Babel in an effort to reach heaven. In his wrath, God sowed disorder into human language and halted the foolish enterprise in its tracks, since the workmen were no longer able to understand one another and abandoned the site. The first utopia was dead in the water. As Gilles Lapouge confirms: "The oldest utopia is that of Babel, and God, by striking down the tower, was simply indicating, at the beginning of time, his position as regards utopia: he is against."

Over succeeding centuries, the Tower of Babel was depicted in painting very frequently. Artists took as their model the ziggurats of Babylon that Herodotus, in the fifth century BCE, describes as follows: "In the middle stands a massive tower, tall and a *stadium* wide, surmounted by another tower which supports a third and so on, up to eight. An external slope spirals up to the final tower."

Pieter Bruegel, The Tower of Babel, 1563. Kunsthistorisches Museum, Vienna, Austria.

Here myth and reality fuse to nourish the dreams of men and of filmmakers—such as Fritz Lang with *Metropolis* (for the construction of the Tower) and Alejandro González Iñárritu with *Babel* (for the hodgepodge of languages)—in particular. And then architects, too, with Vladimir Tatlin's 1919 design for a monument to the glory of the Third International in Moscow, whose form is indeed reminiscent of a Babylonian ziggurat and the object of which was, perhaps, to bring our confusion to an end. But there again, the "little god of the people" did not authorize its construction.

In contemporary architecture, two examples are already legendary. In 1988, François Geindre, the mayor of Hérouville-Saint-Clair (a "new town" created ex nihilo in 1961 in the suburbs of Caen), met Massimiliano Fuksas when on a trip to Rome and asked him to design a landmark to raise the town's profile. "I'll give you a tower," the architect replied, "but I won't do it alone." Fuksas soon got together with Englishman William Alsop, Frenchman Jean Nouvel, and German Otto Steidle.

In an atmosphere of fun and risk, the four joined forces in the design. The result was a three-storey rocket complete with launch pad. Its objective: the sky. The myth of Babel was not dead. First off, Fuksas, with a strange war machine, half robot chock-a-block with cogs, half medieval attack tower, with room for offices; above this, Steidle placed the homes, drenched in light with footbridges and gangways aplenty, in a nod to Le Corbusier; Nouvel's two crowning cylindrical, silo-like towers boasting a hotel, a bar, and a panoramic restaurant; at the base of the rocket tower, Alsop made the vertical horizontal, with stores and a gigantic birdcage that would have been like a hand stretched out to the rest of the town.

The following year, 1989, Jean Nouvel unveiled his project for a "Tour sans Fins" at

La Défense, Paris. The "s" added to the word *fin* (to give "tower without ends") is highly significant: without beginning or end, one might say. The cylinder is 1,380 feet (420 meters) high and 150 feet (45 meters) in diameter. These peculiar statistics would have made it the slimmest high-rise in the world; as straight as an "I," it seems to leap out of the ground and into the heavens. The effect would have been obtained by the opaque black granite at the base morphing first to clear, reflective glass, then to polished aluminum at the perforated summit. An elaborate dialectic that embodies all the major tenets of contemporary architecture: burial and emergence; appearance and disappearance; materiality and immateriality. And, as is only fitting, the tower of Hérouville-Saint-Clair and the Tour sans Fins at La Défense were, like the Tower of Babel and Tatlin's monument, never built.

The curse of Babel lives on.

ABOVE RIGHT
Jean Nouvel, project for the Tour sans Fins, La Défense, Paris, France, 1989.

RIGHT
William Alsop, Massimiliano Fuksas, Jean Nouvel, Otto Steidle, project for a tower for the commune of Hérouville-Saint-Clair, France, 1988.

WHOSE TOWER IS IT ANYWAY?

RIGHT

Daniel Burnham,
Flat Iron Building,
New York, United
States, 1902.

FAR RIGHT

William Pereira,
Transamerica Pyramid,
San Francisco, United
States, 1972.

FACING PAGE

Skidmore, Owings, and
Merry, John Hancock
Center, Chicago, United
States, 1969.

On September 11, 2001, perhaps the curse of Babel seemed once again to have fallen on the Twin Towers of the World Trade Center, built in 1972 at the tip of Manhattan by Minoru Yamasaki.

Barely a century earlier, in 1884, Chicago had kicked off the great high-rise adventure with the Home Insurance Building by William Le Baron Jenney. It was even fitted with elevators! After the great fire that had partly destroyed it, the Windy City began rebuilding and embarked on the conquest of the sky. In 1922, the competition for a building for the Chicago Tribune with a program to erect "the world's most beautiful office building" saw the victory of the New York team of Hood 8 Howells and sparked a deluge of breathtaking plans, signed, among others, by Walter Gropius, Adolf Loos, Bruno Taut, and Eliel Saarinen—the top names of the time.

New York was no slouch, with the erection in 1903 of the incredible Flat Iron Building by Daniel Burnham. Later came the art deco splendor of the Chrysler Building by William Van Alen (1930) and the modernist Gordon Bunshaft's Lever House (1952). Elsewhere one should not forget the Larkin Building built in Buffalo by Frank Lloyd Wright in 1903 whose immense interior cavity prefigures the hotels of John Portman and Norman Foster's Hongkong and Shanghai Bank.

This, then, was the great era of "sky-scrapers," a name which has nothing to do with architecture and all to do with sailing, since a skyscraper is originally a triangular sail raised at the top of the mainmast, where it can, as it were, scrape the sky.

A French author of the period, Louis-Ferdinand Céline, told of his trip to New York in *Journey to the End of Night*: "Just imagine. That city was standing absolutely erect. New York was a standing city … In our part of the world cities lie along the sea coast or on rivers, they recline on the landscape." Indeed Europe had to wait until after the Second World War to see its first towers leaping into the sky: in Amiens in 1952, there came Auguste Perret's tower; in Milan in 1958, the Torre Velasca by BBPR; then, in 1960, the Pirelli Tower by Gio Ponti, the founder of the journal *Domus*; in Copenhagen, in 1960, Arne Jacobsen's SAS Royal Hotel; and in Paris the Croulebarbe Tower by Albert, Boileau, and Labourdette in 1961.

Then, in 1966, to the west of Paris, the Tour Nobel (since renamed the Tour Initiale) by Jean de Mailly and Jacques Depussé, with a facade designed and realized by Jean Prouvé, the first tower at La Défense, which has remained unequaled for its elegance, thrust, and beauty. At the time, a quarrel was brewing that has only recently calmed down concerning the use of the plinth. A tower spouting out of the ground as in New York forms an integral part of the city and therefore of the life of the city. A tower seated on a plinth, as in Paris, isolates itself from the city and therefore dehumanizes it.

The Flat Iron Building is the granddaddy of them all. Although it was built in New York, it is very "Chicago School" and, with superimposed orders up to 285 feet (87 meters) tall, remains historicist in style. In 1969, the Hancock Center, with a height of 41,129 feet (344 meters) (1,499 feet [457 meters] if one counts the antenna on the top), was the tallest tower in the world (in 2009 it is no more than the fourth highest in the United States and the twenty-first in the world). As for the Transamerica Pyramid, lambasted when built in 1972, it is accepted today, with the Golden Gate Bridge, as a symbol of San Francisco.

Today, in response to the galloping rise in population and to hugely increased urban density (the projection for 2020 is five billion urbanites against a total of three billion in the country), building high-rises is more than just an exploit: it has become a necessity. That we have to build higher to forestall urban sprawl as in Mumbai and Mexico City, in Beijing and São Paulo, Tokyo and Kinshasa, is self-evident.

Europe is coming to terms with this, as efforts in London, Rotterdam, Vienna, Warsaw, Madrid, and Barcelona show. Everything is now in place to solve the attendant structural, technical, and material problems. Similarly, problems related to function, density, and polyvalence can be overcome in detailed schedules.

Now, though, the challenges lie elsewhere. First of all, the bid to go ever higher, as a succession of records has fallen like dominos: which will be highest? Then there's ecology, as very tall buildings are massive energy consumers and carbon dioxide-emitters. The goal here is to attain a level of self-sufficiency capable of producing part, or even the totality of the energy consumed, as well as to reduce capital costs and overheads. Finally one must not lose sight of the symbolic import of architecture, since it still has to articulate and express a certain meaning.

In this connection, computing and technological control has made feasible every form of expression, every idiom, every style, every daring plan. To be convinced of the fact, it is enough to gaze on Santiago Calatrava's corkscrews in Malmö, Zaha Hadid's ballet in Dubai, Christian de Portzamparc's folds in Lille, C. Y. Lee's "revival" style in Taipei, Johnson-Burgee's slopes and slants in Madrid, Dominique Perrault's arrhythmia in Barcelona, the false "twins" of Coop Himmelb(l)au in Frankfurt, Rem Koolhaas's strange interpretation of the Möbius strip and the Ark of the Covenant in Beijing, Norman Foster's fun yet wondrous London "Gherkin," or Jean Nouvel's "Missile" in Barcelona.

RIGHT
Ieoh Ming Pei, Bank of China, Hong Kong, China, 1989.

FACING PAGE, TOP LEFT
Christian de Portzamparc, Crédit Lyonnais Tower, Lille, France, 1995.

FACING PAGE, BOTTOM LEFT
Dominique Perrault, the leaning towers of the 3 and the 4* Hotels, Milan, Italy, 2008.*

FACING PAGE, CENTER
C. Y. Lee, Taipei 101, Taipei, Taiwan, 2004.

FACING PAGE, RIGHT
Santiago Calatrava, Turning Torso Tower, Malmö, Sweden, 2007.

FOLLOWING PAGES
Hong Kong's impressive
skyline in which one
can see the Bank of
China by leoh Pei and in
which nestles Norman
Foster's Hongkong
and Shanghai Bank.

GROUNDBREAKERS

9

GROUNDBREAKERS

9

Although somewhat arbitrary, it is not illogical to state that what is customarily called contemporary architecture—a continuation of modern architecture—kicked off in the mid-1970s, with the fuse being lit in 1977 at the Centre Pompidou. Nevertheless, the twenty years preceding this date saw the erection of structures that were groundbreaking in terms of conceptualization, idiom, or style, as well as regards technological advances. Between 1955 and 1975, such harbingers and key events came thick and fast. Below we detail twelve, particularly significant, examples.

19**55**
sacred
LE CORBUSIER

The curve is the "pack-donkey's way," opined Le Corbusier. However, when aged over sixty, he set aside the straight line and orthogonality in his designs for this chapel. Here, the organic unseats modernism; emotion unsettles theory. A declared atheist, Le Corbusier let himself be overcome by a sense of the sacred and surrendered to the lyrical and the uncanny. Though relatively small, from the outside the chapel appears monumental. The intersecting lines, the tangle of right angles and curves, seem to make the structure seem larger. Paradoxically, Notre-Dame-du-Haut only betrays its real scale from the inside, where it reveals an intimate space conducive to meditation.

Notre-Dame-du-Haut Chapel Ronchamp, France

1958
tour de force
ROBERT CAMELOT
JEAN DE MAILLY
BERNARD ZEHRFUSS

The new district of La Défense to the west of Paris had only just started to rise out of the ground when a trio of architects, aided and abetted by two engineers (Nicolas Esquillan for the structure and Jean Prouvé for the facades), performed a miracle: a strange, triangular reinforced-concrete vault spanning some 715 feet (218 meters). An unprecedented, staggering feat. The five coconspirators had all long been at home with concrete, but on this occasion they knew they were demanding more of the material than it was accustomed to providing. To achieve their ends, they devised a technology based on thin, double shells, stiffened by struts, similar to that used in airplane wings.

Fifty years on and the CNIT remains as fresh as the day it was built.

CNIT (Center for New Industries and Technologies) Paris, La Défense, France

19**59**
paradox
FRANK LLOYD WRIGHT

Aged ninety, the foremost American architect was putting the finishing touches to a final work which was inaugurated on October 21, 1959, six months after his death. A masterpiece of space, the museum is also a mass of paradoxes. A dense, solid, imposing building, it is, however, utterly dedicated to movement, like a gigantic snail's shell uncurling around a vast central well. To the normal approach of a series of exhibition halls, Wright preferred a long, spiraling slope that gently climbs to a height of six floors. A museum without picture rails—or almost—its permanent exhibition features little more than 3 percent of the six thousand works or so contained in the collection.

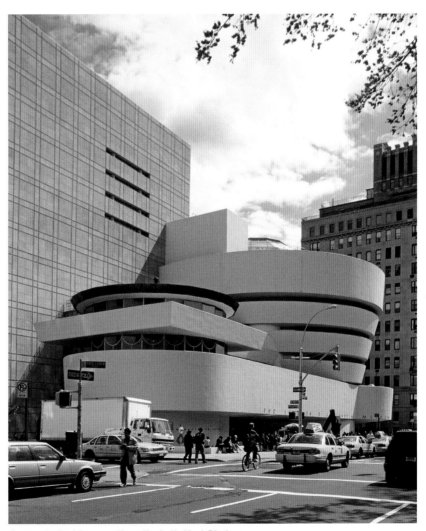

Guggenheim Museum New York, United States

1963
asymmetry
HANS SCHAROUN

Surely Scharoun's most complex and daring structure, this venue attracts architects from the world over to Berlin. One of the city's many landmarks, the Philharmonie offers a wholly different face from the interior, with an orchestra pit in the center of a hall ringed by seating in the shape of an irregular terrace. "The form of the auditorium was inspired by landscape; it can be imagined as a valley; at the bottom lies the orchestra around which stand terraced vineyards. The ceiling forms a celestial landscape corresponding to this earthly landscape," Scharoun confided. And, from the depths of this world there rises, incomparable, the sounds that fall from all sides onto the listeners below.

Philharmonie Berlin, Germany

1968
oblique
CLAUDE PARENT
PAUL VIRILIO

Two friends, two associates, two different characters. At the begining of the 1960s, Parent and Virilio developed the theory of the "oblique function" that formulated a desire to invent a new conception of space summarized in the phrase: "A diagonal line inscribed on a blank page is a hill, perhaps a mountain, a rise, a descent, fall or ascension." The construction of Sainte-Bernadette-du-Banlay was to be the tangible representation of their manifesto. The double masses of a reinforced-concrete shell without windows confront one another like inverted slopes, thereby generating floors in a V-shape, turning the space into a network through which visitors pass. This actualization of vertigo recurs later in other works, in particular with the deconstructivists, and especially in Berlin's Jewish Museum by Daniel Libeskind, whose ramps seem to illustrate the oblique function.

Sainte-Bernadette-du-Banlay Nevers, France

1968
color
LUIS BARRAGÁN

The rigorous geometry, metaphysical dimension, and abstract formal vocabulary, as well as the preeminence allotted to enclosed spaces by Luis Barragán, the great Mexican architect, give rise to structures of ineffable beauty. It is a tenuous, retrained species of beauty, brought to life by the transfiguring, transcendent deployment of color and light. Modest yet lyrical pieces at whose core lies an obvious and indeed acknowledged Moorish influence. The unspoken dialogues created by Barragán between the sun and his hallmark blind walls, magnified by the omnipresence of water, reach an apogee in his residential complexes and equestrian country clubs (he was an inveterate horseman), of which Los Clubes is surely the most accomplished.

Cuadra San Cristóbal, Los Clubes Mexico City, Mexico

19**71**
lyricism
JØRN UTZON

Australia came to love architecture thanks to a Dane. It was Utzon who, in 1957, won the competition for the Sydney Opera House, though it was inaugurated sixteen years later, completed by other hands. But the Opera House is indeed the creation of Utzon, whose architectural language draws its laws from nature.

The 1950s had a penchant for rigor. And yet Utzon, the son of a naval architect, was prepared to make room for lyricism and moored in the port of Sydney a concrete vessel whose sails form a nest of monumental shells that seem to open like a flower. Supporting these shells, an immense stepped platform generates a striking public space. The whole is carried on 580 concrete pillars hammered in 82 feet (25 meters) below sea level, and is illuminated by a central canopy roof more than 112 feet (34 meters) high suspended without intermediate supports.

Sydney Opera House Australia

1972
exploit
ROGER TAILLIBERT

The Parc des Princes stadium is a great concrete beast that spans the ring road on the border between Paris and Boulogne. This gigantic ellipsis is fixed on cantilevered gantries that encircle the whole, and which appear to be identical but are actually thirteen different coexisting modules. The stadium sits beneath a great hood, similarly elliptical, whose corbelling extends some 164 feet (50 meters). It is an obvious technical tour de force—the prestressed concrete genuinely under stress has to be subdued; but it is also a feat of spatial control, as the structure's monumental exterior gives way to a feeling of closeness within. Finally, it shows aesthetic brilliance in its synthesis of idioms (classical, expressionist, constructivist, organicist) that, together, produce an absolutely new story in which it is impossible to tell, out of form and function, which has generated which.

Parc des Princes stadium Paris, France

1972
lightness
FREI OTTO

There was a sharp intake of breath on the day the Munich Olympic Games opened. High above the Olympic stadium, the roof seemed impossibly light: one record had already been broken. Like a huge, bubbling, translucent wave, it looked ready to shoot into the sky. Once more, Frei Otto had demonstrated—this time in the eyes of the whole world—his mastery of suspension structures, of thin, synthetic membranes fixed with slender steel-wire ropes clamped to masts of variable heights. Inspired by the sport of gliding of which he was especially fond, the structure's outline already hints at bionic architecture with its natural forms, curved surfaces, fractals, etc., as well as prefiguring future economical solutions in its systematic search for optimum results through the use of the least materials and effort.

Olympic Stadium Munich, Germany

19**74**
silence
LOUIS KAHN

Louis Kahn was a man of silence, as demonstrated in *My Architect*, the film about him made by his son Nathaniel that explores his father's four discrete lives. The same applies to his architecture, some of the most important and accomplished of all time. Relying on contrast and opposition, juxtaposing materials and forms, Kahn provides a masterful recapitulation of the modern movement that he crystallized into a measured yet captivating body of work. His National Assembly in Dacca shows his supreme control of this "silence." Though secular, Kahn's architecture extols the purest formal harmony and is essentially mystical, thoughtful, and meditative.

National Assembly Dacca, Bangladesh

1975
heresy
SITE

Founded in New York in the early 1970s, the SITE group was a joint venture between four talents—Alison Sky, Emilio Sousa, Michelle Stone, and James Wines—artists rather than architects. For the Best Products chain, SITE came up with a series of strange, intriguingly named locales: Peel Project (1972), in Richmond, Virginia; Indeterminate Facade (1975) in Houston, Texas; Notch Project (1977) in Sacramento, California; Tilt Showroom (1978) in Towson, Maryland; and Cutler Ridge Showroom (1979) in Miami, Florida—all of which seem either unfinished or in the process of being demolished. These (pre-)ruined creations pre-empt and embrace the vicissitudes of time: a kind of ne plus ultra of architecture, they juggle irony and paradox, clarity and planned obsolescence. Some may be comical and others visionary, but all are artistic: with the Forest Showroom (1980), again for Best, in Richmond, Virginia, their humorous approach offers a new take on the paradigms of ecology and green architecture, with results both heretical and realistic—as one might expect.

Indeterminate Facade, Best Store Houston, United States

10

10

ALVAR AALTO

A hero of modernity—certainly! In terms of dates, however, Alvar Aalto belongs to modern rather than to contemporary architecture. However, conscious of the limits of rigid and austere functionalism and eschewing systematic recourse to orthogonal forms, he permitted curved and diagonal lines suggestive of a continuous space. Subtle articulations were created through a poetics of form and space and enhanced by contrasted deployment of various materials: brick, different types of timber, slate, and marble, as well as copper for roofs.

In each structure, he displays a masterly handling of asymmetry and incomparable freedom in planning, poetic intuition, and an organic sense of ordered integration. The corrugated walls and staircases that ripple along the facades of the hall of residence of the Massachusetts Institute of Technology (1949) offer a perfect illustration.

With the Helsinki conference center and concert hall, known as the Finlandia, Aalto attained supreme stylistic unity, together with an attention to detail and a sensual treatment of materials that are second to none. Bordering the Bay of Töölönlahti and backing on to Hesperia Park, the Finlandia, clad entirely in plates of white Carrara marble, floats like a vast liner ready to set sail. The congress hall is counterbalanced by a large auditorium for an audience of 1,700 and a room for chamber concerts. The three sites are connected through a large, light-filled foyer facing out over the lake.

The vast auditorium, fan-shaped and enlivened with great waves of white, is not just a visual delight but also a masterpiece of acoustics. So what is Aalto? Classical, modern, visionary, contemporary? No: Just timeless!

major works

1933 **Sanatorium,** Paimio, Finland ✪ 1939 **Villa Mairea,** Noormarkku, Finland ✪ 1964 **Opera house,** Essen, Germany ✪ 1966 **Helsinki University of Technology campus,** Otaniemi, Finland ✪ 1972 **Museum of Modern Art,** Aalborg, Denmark ✪ 1978 **Parish center,** Riola di Vergato, Italy

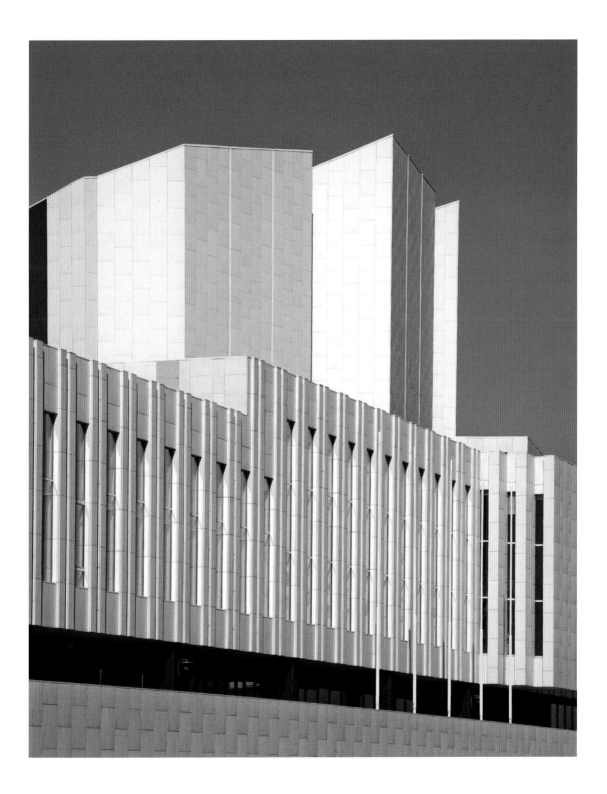

VITO ACCONCI

As the 1970s dawned, New York was a vibrant, bubbling place. A new generation of artists was coming into prominence and would view the world in a whole new way. The opening in 1971 in Chelsea of The Kitchen, a meeting place and venue for performance art, was to fuse them into a group. Night after night, Steve Reich, Philip Glass, Gary Hill, Lucinda Childs, Charles Atlas, Laurie Anderson, Bill T. Jones, Brian Eno, Cindy Sherman, and Meredith Monk strutted their stuff. These musicians, choreographers, poets, and visual and video artists, all unknowns at the time, were soon to mark the history of art, in all its forms.

Among them was a young poet who had already published short stories in the notorious *Olympia* magazine and had just founded the review *0 to 9*. Acconci was clearly already receptive to the tactile nature of the world, since he laid his pages out like small-scale performance spaces. Very quickly, he moved toward photography, soundworks, and video, before becoming a significant performance artist, exploring real, temporal, social, and cultural space by placing his own and his audience's body at the heart of the action.

Continuing his explorations, Acconci now directed his researches toward installation and environmental art, the logical upshot being the founding, in 1988, of the Acconci Studio where he was surrounded by artists and architects. Pursuing his quest still further, he showed increasing concern with architecture and urban development, producing a number of projects related to parks and adventure playgrounds. Very few were actually realized, but their impact was of consequence for many artists, architects, and landscape architects.

In 2007, an unidentified floating object was spotted in Graz. This was the Murinsel ("island on the Mur"), landing delicately on the river that runs through the Austrian city. Here Acconci tries to show how an urban space might be treated as open forum, debating chamber, and discussion platform. The Murinsel is a walkway that is also a hybrid structure linking the two banks of the watercourse over a pair of slender footbridges, the shell of which contains a metal-and-glass café, a theater with seating for 200, and a children's play area. Generated by the distortion of a double geodesic dome, the Murinsel, as liquid as the waters beneath, is a successful example of the osmosis between art and architecture.

WILLIAM ALSOP

A forest of tall steel struts crowned by a long rectangle parallelepiped with white skin, dotted, pixelated in black, resembling an enormous and menacing species of arachnid. One is unsure whether this gigantic vessel is delicately stepping over the long, rust-colored building it looks down on or getting ready to crush it to a pulp. The resulting sensation is strange. But the vessel remains motionless, and the long red diagonal inscribed on its underside accentuates a mystery tailor-made to excite the imagination of any self-respecting psychoanalyst.

This futuristic extravagance linking the two buildings, a mysterious block box that the Kubrick of *2001: A Space Odyssey*, would not have been ashamed of, is the solution to the task of restructuring and extending the space of the Ontario College of Art 8 Design in Toronto arrived at by William Alsop, whose taste for unusual forms and saturated colors is well-known. If the exterior is a striking performance, the interior is none the less so, the architect proposing a triumphant unity between the two spaces, old and new, through the deployment of lights and colors showing up against the omnipresent white. From Toronto to London, via West Bromwich, Alsop's work is like a harbinger of some future civilization.

major works

1984 Swimming pool, Norfolk, United Kingdom ✱ **1985 Cardiff Bay Visitor Center,** Cardiff, United Kingdom ✱ **1994 Seat of regional government,** Marseille, France ✱ **2000 Peckham Library,** South London, United Kingdom ✱ **2005 Ben Pimlott Building,** University of London, United Kingdom ✱ **2008 The Public,** West Bromwich, United Kingdom

TADAO ANDO

For the creator of so many churches, chapels, and places of meditation, the words "Church of Light" were essential to Tadao Ando's trajectory. His architecture, in which one feels the indubitable presence of both Le Corbusier and Louis Kahn, exalts spirituality though pure forms born of a rigorous geometry where line, circle, and square dominate. These are abstract spaces in which nature (air, water, earth) fuses with culture (architecture), the preferred material being concrete, treated so as to unmistakably evoke skin, a living, breathing outer coating which reacts divinely to the light. This is essential Ando. His entire architectural oeuvre is centered on the subtle play of light worked as paint so that it literally covers the walls. The concern is as much with spirituality as with a beauty as touching as it is restrained, tenuous. And there can be no better demonstration than the Church of Light itself, built early in this autodidact's career. A space at the same time lyrical and modest, with a cross hewn out of the concrete wall and projected onto the floor, filling the whole with an unexpected blaze of light. An architecture of silence for a place of meditation.

major works
1991 Vitra Conference Pavilion, Weil-am-Rhein, Germany ✸ **1992 Japanese Pavilion for Expo 92,** Seville, Spain ✸ **1998 Modern Art Museum of Fort Worth,** United States ✸ **2003 4x4 House,** Kobe, Japan ✸ **2004 Chichu Art Museum,** Naoshima, Japan ✸ **2006 and 2008 Palazzo Grassi and Punta della Dogana,** François Pinault Foundation, Venice, Italy

SHIGERU BAN

Paper, paperboard, bamboo, textiles, and plywood are the favorite materials of Shigeru Ban, who has won a reputation as the all-weight champion of low-tech and economy of means. His approach proceeds from a twofold interest in and commitment to ethics and ecology. In all his structures, be they public or private, he strives to establish a dialogue with nature in spaces largely open to the elements.

His Curtain Wall House is the best-known and most attractive example. As a committed architect, Ban reacted to the earthquake that devastated Kobe in 1995 with lightning speed, developing emergency housing with his students called "paper loghouses." These were 172-sqaure foot (16-square meters) shelters made of cardboard tubes 4 inches (11 centimeters) in diameter seated on foundations cobbled together from Kirin beer cases emptied and ballasted with sand that could be mounted or dismantled in an instant, while the roof was just recycled tent fabric. These "paper log-houses" were taken up eagerly in Japan and elsewhere in Asia, as well as in Africa—every place in fact where emergency housing became a necessity. It is a simple yet brilliant idea implemented through an alternative pattern of thinking that is ethical as much as economic and that combines waste avoidance with recycling. In this unexpectedly effective yet elegant emergency dwelling, Ban shows that if imagination is seldom in power, the power of the imagination at least has no limits.

major works

1995 **Paper House,** Lake Yamanaka, Japan ❈ 1995 **Curtain Wall House,** Tokyo, Japan ❈ 1999 **Nemunoki Children's** Art Museum, Shizuoka, Japan ❈ 2000 **Naked House,** Kawagoe, Japan ❈ 2002 **Nomadic Museum,** Venice, Italy, followed by New York in 2005, Santa Monica in 2007, Paris in 2009 ❈ 2009 **Centre-Pompidou-Metz,** France

PATRICK BOUCHAIN

At the gates of Paris, yards from the French national stadium, the Stade de France, in a kind of no-man's land of waste ground, brownfield sites, disused factories, and film and television studios, there stands a sort of barn flanked by four huge red warts to which a multicolored ballet of people from all over the world comes in droves whenever it's open. The Académie Fratellini is a circus school Patrick Bouchain treated, as is his habit, in an extremely pragmatic way, with no aesthetic hallmarks, no systematic formalism, and no pet materials. "To do the least possible to provide as much as possible," affirms the architect, who always endeavors to deliver the most effective amenities with the greatest economy of means.

Rather than being dwarfed by some showy or costly structure, at the Académie Fratellini, nomads and travelers, wanderers and part-timers, people of movement and the road, traveling entertainers and troupes all immediately feel at home. Out of practically nothing, Bouchain produces settings for other disciplines and other territories, instead of a showcase for his own. He does it here, in the Académie Fratellini; as well as in the equestrian theater of Zingaro, the Volière Dromesko theater, in the urban interventions by Daniel Buren, and, with Rostropovich, in the Grange au Lac, an auditorium for the music festival at Evian.

major works

1984 **Centre d'Art Contemporain Le Magasin,** Grenoble, France ✹ 1988 **Théâtre Zingaro,** Aubervilliers, France ✹ 1997 **Headquarters, Thomson Multimedia,** Boulogne-Billancourt, France ✹ 1999 **Conversion of the Lu factory into the Lieu Unique,** Nantes, France ✹ 2005 **Les Bains, municipal swimming pool,** Bègles, France ✹ 2007 **Cité Nationale de l'Histoire de l'Immigration,** Paris, France

COOP HIMMELB(L)AU

Depending on whether you read it "Himmelbau" or "Himmelblau," it means either "building the sky/heaven" or, more simply, "sky blue." The two celestial conspirators-cum-cooperators from Vienna, Helmut Swiczinsky and Wolf D. Prix, have definitively opted for building. Even though they met in the 1970s, in the heyday of the paper utopias, it was only in 1988, at the *Deconstructivist Architecture* show curated by Philip Johnson at MoMA that they came to public notice. And it is true that their architecture, with its daring geometry, tangential lines, adventurous diagonals, sculptural and tumultuous forms, and its bristling, aggressive expressiveness, belongs more to the aleatory, to energy, to dislocation and outburst, than to the realm of order and reason; a kind of "automatic writing," composed with eyes shut tight, so that no idea gets away.

For the Dresden film complex they produced two interlocking blocks: the first, unyielding in its opaque concrete, seems to have been placed on an apex and houses eight projection rooms; the second is a faceted glass prism enclosing an 15-foot (35-meter) high atrium, transparent so as to leave exposed a tangle of suspended staircases, of slopes spanning the abyss, of swaying walkways. As an extra, standing opposite the city, a metal facade overhung by a massive cantilever. The whole is sliced through by a public passageway that serves as a link between two streets and three of the city's districts. A kind of nodal space, it points out and up the urban fabric of Dresden—a city flattened at the end of the Second World War and hastily rebuilt with dreadful results. In its antagonism, this form revives and amplifies the urban tension of its nondescript environment, bringing it—quite simply—to life.

major works

1994 **Extension to the Groningen Museum,** The Netherlands ✺ 2001 **Gasometer B,** Vienna, Austria ✺ 2005 **Akademie der Bildenden Künste,** Munich, Germany ✺ 2006 **Akron Art Museum,** United States ✺ 2007 **BMW Welt,** Munich, Germany ✺ 2009 **Musées des Confluences,** Lyon, France

NORMAN FOSTER

To the right, the Causse de Saint-Affrique. To the left, the Causse de Larzac. And deep, deep down, ensconced in the valley far below, the meandering, snaking River Tarn. From the summit of the viaduct, the view over this wild beauty is breathtaking. From distant Creissels, the sight is hardly less extraordinary. But out here, this time, it is well worth raising one's eyes to look at the structure carving a path through the sky. Beauty resides there too; self-evident, unforgiving, razor-sharp, a structural beauty so overwhelming that it almost makes one forget about the quality of the design, of the archi-tectural writing. It is reminiscent of one of those structures without an architect, like the Roman Pont du Gard, which also seems to emerge naturally from the landscape, or of an engineering feat like Gustave Eiffel's Garabit Viaduct in the Pyrenees, with all its symbolic power. In Millau, patently, the symbiosis between nature and culture, between architect and engineer, is seamless and harmonious. The result is a long, airy curve, standing on seven majestic piers supporting an apron some 8,070 feet (2,460 meters) long and 98 feet (30 meters) wide, the whole dominated by seven pylons trussed with 154 steel shrouds. In total some 319,700 tons of steel and concrete: and yet the feeling is of incredible light-ness. With this viaduct that disdains all norms, Foster once again shows his technological virtuosity, the care lavished on the tiniest detail, his drive for efficiency. Towering above Millau, all equations resolve into the golden number.

major works

1986 **Headquarters of the Hongkong and Shanghai Bank,** Hong Kong, China ✱ 1998 **Carré d'Art,** Nîmes, France ✱ 1999 **Reichstag Dome,** Berlin, Germany ✱ 2002 **Sage Music Center,** Gateshead, United Kingdom ✱ 2004 **Swiss Re Tower,** London, United Kingdom ✱ 2008 **Beijing Airport,** China

MASSIMILIANO FUKSAS

It requires no great foresight to call Massimiliano Fuksas a baroque architect, an "architect who walks," enamored of urban settings, with movement, with combining genres, with grammar, technique, and material, who risks the "oblique" as well as the deconstructive, never doing the same thing twice, always popping up where he is least expected, and forever asserting that art and architecture form a whole, that they are but one.

In Niaux in the Pyrenees, there is a cave containing paintings of wondrous beauty and great rarity dating back to the Magdalenian Paleolithic culture. Fuksas's account was to erect an entrance to regulate visitor flow and protect the site. A seemingly minor project which Fuksas would turn into a major masterpiece in his own inimitable fashion. The entryway to the cave is framed by two titanic wings 92 feet (28 meters) high, fastened firmly to pilotis that plunge down 82 feet (25 meters) into the rock. Two huge wings which do not touch the mountain but which are able to resist violent winds. The superstructure dives into the cavern, preparing us for the revelation within through a sort of initiation course. A frenzied dialogue between red cedar and pre-patinated rust-colored steel echoes the rock-face, while the reception building itself threads beneath the long steel and wood pier. The architect here swaps his favorite urban scene-setting for a telluric one not without baroque emphasis, a kind of primary structure in the manner of a Richard Serra that embraces the topos in the manner of a Carl Andre. Its violence and passion are clear for all to see. To stand before this splendid bird, outsized and awe-inspiring and ready to take flight, is to be bowled over.

major works

1991 **Médiathèque**, Rezé, France ✳ 1996 **Îlot Candie**, Paris, France ✳ 2001 **Vienna Twin Towers**, Vienna, Austria ✳ 2004 **Ferrari Research Center**, Maranello, Italy ✳ 2005 **Fiera Milano Exhibition Complex**, Milan, Italy ✳ 2008 **Zénith (music hall)**, Strasbourg, France

FUTURE SYSTEMS

What can this be? In the uninspiring district of the Bullring on the edges of Birmingham city center there broods a kind of gigantic insect carapaced in thousands of chrome aluminum discs resembling chainmail links.

This curious mix of heroic fantasy and science fiction, this amorphous and organic form, an illustration of "blobitecture," couples the utopian pipe-dreams of the 1970s (the Archigram tendency) to the pragmatism of high-tech (the Foster-Rogers tendency). This patently bionic and no less obviously British architecture springs from the fertile imagination of a tandem made up of the Czech, Jan Kaplický, and the Englishwoman, Amanda Levete. Faced with this outlandish shell that seems to invite one on more than just a shopping trip and out to the borders of deep space, it's hard to decide whether it's a shopping center or a spaceship, department store or phantasmagoric animal. Exploding like a firework in the sunshine, reverberating under the rain, gleaming come nightfall, Future Systems' Selfridges looks like a cottony cocoon or an eye of a thousand facets peering out. The eye is, moreover, a recurrent theme in their work: the media center in Lord's Cricket Ground also looks ocular, and the entrances to their Comme des Garçons boutiques resemble optic nerves.

FRANK O. GEHRY

The industrial city of Bilbao had been dormant for a long time. Its factories deserted, hit by an economic recession and galloping unemployment, it was on the ropes. The Guggenheim Museum was to wake it up and transform it into a tourist hub. An architectural masterstroke by Frank O. Gehry and Thomas Krens, the enterprising head of the Solomon R. Guggenheim Foundation, morphed into a symptom, an accelerator, a brand, in the business sense of the term.

The New York Guggenheim, a wondrous creation by Frank Lloyd Wright, is world-famous, as is Peggy Guggenheim's delectable *palazzetto* beached on the edges of the Grand Canal. Gehry's Guggenheim heralded the "Bilbao effect": a project at once architectural and economic that was to effect tourism and society—a concrete symbol of globalization.

A fun-loving organic monster, a fragmented farrago of volumes, with stone-dressed regular forms, and violent, curved forms clad in titanium plating, the whole punctuated by great glazed walls. One encounters, upon entering, two breathtaking spaces of gigantic size: an immense room without columns, 427 feet (130 meters) long by 98 feet (30 meters) wide, designed for blockbuster shows (such as Richard Serra's primary structures at the opening), and an equally enormous atrium from which branches out a system of curved footbridges, glazed elevators, and staircase towers connecting the nineteen galleries of the museum, all in different shapes and sizes.

In Bilbao the expertise Gehry has shown in obliging the folded, pleated, and scrunched forms of his models and sketches to coexist with the most powerful software—and thus to subject IT to the imagination and technology to art—is once again plain for all to see.

major works
1989 **Vitra Design Museum,** Weil-am-Rhein, Germany ✿ 1993 **Frederick R. Weisman Art Museum,** Minneapolis, United States ✿ 1999 **Der Neue Zollhof quarter,** Düsseldorf, Germany ✿ 2000 **DG Bank Building,** Berlin, Germany ✿ 2003 **Walt Disney Concert Hall,** Los Angeles, United States ✿ 2006 **Marqués de Riscal Hotel,** Elciego, Spain

ZAHA HADID

Dominating the mountain and zigzagging through the sky like an immense Z: Has Zorro's "Z" upped sticks from its native California and landed in Austria? No, "Z" stands for Zaha! For the black-clad Zaha Hadid, she of the breakneck career, an architect who overcomes all obstacles with energy and assuredness.

A Londoner born in Baghdad, or a Baghdadi living and working in London, she is to date the only female winner of the Mies van der Rohe Prize (2003) and the Pritzker Prize (2004), and is listed by *Forbes* magazine as the sixty-eigth most influential woman in the world.

Coming to prominence in 1988 at the *Deconstructive Architecture* exhibition at New York's MoMA, where she rubbed shoulders with Coop Himmelb(l)au, Eisenman, Gehry, Koolhaas, Libeskind, and Tschumi, on many occasions since she has amply demonstrated her virtuosity, mastery of chaos, fondness for exploding forms, joyous expression of tension, as well as her highly personal talent for riding roughshod over established codes and her penchant for interlacing stressed curves and lines, for overlapping planes and cantilevers. The result: structures sharpened to points like diamonds, fractured like icebergs, with razor-sharp graphic lines, streaked and aggressive.

No more than a century ago, on February 20, 1909, in *Le Figaro*, Filippo Tommaso Marinetti published his "Futurist Manifesto" that affirmed: "We declare that the splendor of the world has been enriched by a new beauty, the beauty of speed." Speed, movement, violence, provocation, polemics—it seems that this is also Zaha Hadid's chosen habitat, as testified by her ski jump in Innsbruck, whose sculptural form mixing tension and torsion seems born from a hybrid between tower and bridge. And up there, accessible via a pair of elevators, perches a café from which the view over the landscape and the competitors below is incomparable.

major works

1993 **Vitra Fire Station,** Weil-am-Rhein, Germany ✺ 2001 **Tram station,** Strasbourg, France ✺ **Lois & Richard Rosenthal Center for Contemporary Art,** Cincinnati, United States ✺ 2005 **BMW Central Building,** Leipzig, Germany ✺ 2008 **Phaeno Scientific Center,** Wolfsburg, Germany ✺ 2009 **MAXXI National Museum of 21st Century Arts,** Rome, Italy

HERZOG & DE MEURON

Face to face, on either side of the Thames, stand Christopher Wren's Saint Paul's Cathedral and the Bankside electric power station by Giles Gilbert Scott. The cathedral is still there, immutable, eternal. The power station had been out of commission since 1983. Seventeen years of silence and inactivity ensued during which this mass of brick and its two enormous chimney-stacks appeared in the background of countless movies, videos, postcards, and album covers. And then, in 2000, the old monster stirred from its slumber to become the bustling Tate Modern, the most "arty" place in London, converted, renovated, and revamped by the Swiss architectural tandem of Herzog 8 de Meuron. The schedule combined a complete overhaul with featherlight retouching. The gigantic turbine hall was re-planned as a dizzying reception area and the boiler rooms turned into a receptacle for seven floors housing galleries, bookshops, and cafés, light-filled boxes that overhang the main nave and are lit with neons of various hues.

Still higher above, on the power station's flat roof, a long, illuminated strut contains two further storeys with display halls and a panoramic restaurant from where the view is breathtaking. Seldom can contemporary art have been showcased as in Tate Modern. It should though be recalled that Herzog 8 de Meuron have always had close links with contemporary art (the Swiss artist Rémy Zaugg was a long-term collaborator). Once again, they demonstrate their subtle and intricate use of space, their command of technology and movement, of material and evanescence. In 2005 the architects were appointed to develop plans for the extension of Tate Modern and its immediate surroundings tabled for 2012.

major works
1994 **SBB Switch Tower,** Basel, Switzerland ✸ **2000** **Apartment building,** rue des Suisses, Paris, France ✸ **2003** **Schaulager, Laurenz-Stiftung,** Basel/Münchenstein, Switzerland ✸ **2005** **Allianz Arena,** Munich, Germany ✸ **2008** **Caixa Forum,** Madrid, Spain ✸ **2008** **TEA, Tenerife Espacio de las Artes,** Santa Cruz de Tenerife, Spain

TOYO ITO

From the exterior, and at night even more than in the daytime, the Sendai Mediatheque vibrates like a body of fluid, like an organic membrane. On three of its faces, great double-walled glass screens transform this biomorphic structure into a magic lantern, while the perforated aluminum plating on the fourth side and the steel on the roof provide solidity. From the outside, too, the purpose of the building is not immediately obvious, the space being vertically traversed by thirteen seemingly haphazard luminous beams (in fact thirteen tubular-steel columns containing the power supplies and communication and information conduits) that give it a disembodied air. Inside though, various zones take shape, but each story is a different height, while furniture, lighting, and color schemes are equally variable.

The thirteen columns or pillars, each creating its own rhythm of concentric circles, like a stone thrown into a pond, fuel the Sendai Mediatheque with its vital energy and organic drive. Specification and schedule cooperate here with improvised arabesques to forge a fluent syntax that generates ambiguous, marginal readings. Fluidity is essential to Ito as it goes hand in hand with his preference for malleability over monumentality, for the effects of time over the faint hope of longevity. Not afraid of the impalpable and the transitory, exploiting the potential of electronics to the full, Ito's Sendai Mediatheque is a paragon of fluidity and intensity.

major works
1976 **White-U House,** Tokyo (destroyed in 1987), Japan ❋ 1984 **Silver Hut,** Tokyo, Japan ❋ 1988 **Wind Tower,** Yokohama, Japan ❋ 1991 **Municipal Museum,** Yatsushiro, Japan ❋ 2004 **Tod's Building,** Tokyo, Japan ❋ 2005 **Mikimoto Building,** Tokyo, Japan

REM KOOLHAAS

A monster of almost 6,5 million square feet (600,000 square meters), in which more than 10,000 employees work round the clock for a "mere" 250 television companies broadcasting to all the nation and to many cultures and in all the languages that make up the vast jigsaw puzzle that is modern China. The undertaking was no small one. The building had to be ready on time for the Beijing Olympics and be part of the facelift being given to the new China. The schedule was equally demanding, while the competition attracted some of the greatest names in international architecture.

It was Rem Koolhaas who carried the day with a bizarrely shaped skyscraper: it is hard to say whether this sign in space is a tribute to a letter or a pictogram, an impossible italic, an improbable encounter between yin and yang, or the materialization of the notion of exchange. Boasting two towers, it resembles a weird reinterpretation of the Möbius strip or a novel solution to the squaring of the circle. Once again Koolhaas betrays his penchant for taking up the gauntlet, for playing fast and loose, for juggling paradoxes. Over time, he has developed a new alphabet, a new vocabulary, substituting novel and autonomous modalities for the well-worn modes of representation bequeathed by modernity, by all modernities, thereby causing an epistemological schism as violent as the one heralded by cubism in our conception of visual construction over a century ago: his is an exploration of alien spatiality.

With the CCTV Headquaters in Beijing, the Dutch architect exhausts all possible variations in scale, all possible interferences with visibility, all possible strata of legibility.

major works
1991 Nexus World Housing, Fukuoka, Japan, 1991 ✿ **Villa Dall'Ava,** Saint-Cloud, France, 1991 ✿ **1992 Kunsthal,** Rotterdam, The Netherlands ✿ **2001 Casa da Música,** Porto, Portugal ✿ **2003 The Netherlands Embassy,** Berlin, Germany ✿ **2004 Central Library,** Seattle, United States

DANIEL LIBESKIND

A long, broken line, solid concrete, and riveted plates of zinc. The destructuration of a Star of David into a zigzagging slash. In a Jewish Museum, in Berlin, this can be seen as a symbolic, narrative gesture generated by abstraction and geometry. Yet, faced with such radicality and emotion, this is not the feeling one has.

Neither monument nor memorial, this museum results from the endless dialogue between continuity and discontinuity, between presence and absence. A petrified form, precipitating out of fractures and fragmentations, a conflation of complexity and simplicity, where memory and disquiet dog one's every step.

To enter it, to climb down its staircases or shuffle down its slopes, to glimpse the daylight through apertures resembling loopholes, to move on from the pathway of Emigration to the garden of Exile—forty-eight of whose forty-nine pillars are filled with earth from Berlin with the last containing soil from Jerusalem—to move slowly on to the Holocaust Tower, an immense, spare space in which the visitor remains confined for ten minutes, is not unlike a descent into Hell.

The spaces succeed one another discontinuously, "deconstructed" so that they perturb one's sense of direction and arouse sensations of angst experienced as physically as they are mentally. This strategy of the void, of emptiness that the architect develops leads irremediably to the inexpressible.

It is a place that sings and screams at the same time, belonging to a realm far beyond architecture, where word and sound, where literature and music are at their most awesome. For the crux—in this first building by Libeskind, who was then over fifty and who had long worked as a musician, mathematician, and theorist before becoming an architect—resides above all in writing and composition.

major works

2002 **The Imperial War Museum North,** Manchester, United Kingdom ✷ 2003 **Danish Jewish Museum,** Copenhagen, Denmark ✷ 2005 **Wohl Center, University of Bar-Ilan,** Ramat Gan, Israel ✷ 2006 **Extension to the Denver Art Museum,** United States ✷ 2007 **Contemporary Jewish Museum,** San Francisco, United States ✷ 2009 **Military History Museum,** Dresden, Germany

GLENN MURCUTT

So exceptional, so unexpected, and so pregnant with the future are they that it is no easy task to choose just one among the several hundred houses built by Glenn Murcutt. We have selected Nicholas House, since it wonderfully shows the architect's reinterpretation of the codes of his country's vernacular architecture, by employing similar types of plan (long and straight) and materials (especially galvanized corrugated sheeting). Taste and pleasure remain, but without an ounce of the picturesque. The equal, but in a totally different register, Aalto, Chareau, or Mies van der Rohe, Murcutt practices architecture as a modest craftsman, his chief concerns being simplicity, order, and emptiness, so as to weave deep, meaningful interconnections between man and his environment.

Working alone, refusing showy projects, deeply anchored in his beloved Australia, in 2002 he was an unexpected recipient of the Pritzker Prize thanks to his simple, but nevertheless expressive and refined houses that pay tribute to the pared-down, to the "almost nothing," to essence.

Clearly, for Murcutt, an unusual and sincere creator, the absolute reference is nature. This is confirmed by Françoise Fromonot in the fine book she has devoted to his work: "Glenn Murcutt is a militant ecologist. His houses are designed to consume the least possible energy. Once that required for their construction has been consumed, their structure makes them reactive to a wide range of climatic conditions. With humped or raised roofs, with awnings calculated to the nearest millimeter so as to respond to seasonal changes in solar inclination and the situation of the outlook at any given locality, with frontages that can be adjusted to atmospheric variations, and with interiors never deeper than a single room to encourage the movement of fresh air."

A free, liberated, unfettered architecture that never heeds the siren voice of technology and its shortcuts and crutches.

major works

1980 **Marie Short House,** Kempsey, Australia ✸ 1992 **Murcutt Guest Studio,** Kempsey, Australia ✸ 1994 **Simpson-Lee House,** Mount Wilson, Australia ✸ 1994 **Bowali Visitor Information Center,** Kakadu National Park, Australia ✸ 1998 **Fletcher-Page House,** Kangaroo Valley, Australia ✸ 1999 **Arthur and Yvonne Boyd Art Center,** West Cambewarra, Australia

30 ARCHITECTS and their major works

MVRDV

No need to hunt for some pretentious acronym: MVRDV simply stands for the initials of the surnames of its founder members (Winy Maas, Jacob van Rijs, and Nathalie de Vries), and one of the most innovative teams in contemporary architecture.

Preoccupied with problems of development and density, MVRDV's architects have realized a number of residential units exemplifying this approach, particularly important in the Netherlands, where the acquisition of land has long been a struggle. The result is future-centered structures that may adopt unconventional forms but which are not, their authors insist, generated by artistic ambitions. Nevertheless ...

One such, The Dutch Pavilion for Expo 2000 in Hanover, based on the required theme of sustainable development, is edifice and manifesto rolled into one: a superposition of geographical layers, from underground chamber to ecosystem, a landscape of dunes and caves at ground level to a terrace planted with windmills, with four other levels devoted to horticultural activities, to a dense forest of greenery, and to rain.

Like a "Dutch hamburger," it posited the problem of land development in the most radical manner. Open to the four winds, with no facade at all, girded with suspended staircases, the cubic Dutch Pavilion ran through all the accepted doctrine on the subject. A curious oscillation between the playful and transitory nature of construction and the seriousness and urgency of the problems tackled, of density (of development) and artificiality (of the Netherlands). A political architecture, in the most literal sense of the term.

major works

1997 **VVoZoCo Apartments,** Osdorp, The Netherlands ✤ 2003 **Cultural Center,** Matsudai, Japan ✤ 2003 **Silodam,** Amsterdam, The Netherlands ✤ 2004 **Mirador Building,** Madrid, Spain ✤ 2005 **Cancer Center,** Amsterdam, The Netherlands ✤ 2008 **Cleveland Institute of Art,** Cleveland, United States

OSCAR NIEMEYER

In 1967 in a working-class district of Paris smack in the middle of the nineteenth arrondissement, the first attempt to escape the architectural socialist realism that characterizes international Communism took place. In exile in France due to his political convictions, the Brazilian architect designed for the headquarters of what was at the time France's biggest political party a gloriously paradoxical object: modernist, yet undulating; rigorous, yet baroque; open, yet controlled.

Niemeyer's entire architectural vocabulary—of lyricism and spontaneity, of imaginative drive and creative delicacy, of planning simplicity and theatricality, of visual elegance and linear clarity—expresses itself over five floors beneath a garden terrace from which emerges the half-buried dome of the Central Committee. Curve and counter-curve, arch, vault, and slope resonate like a strange score in which the veiled and unveiled vie one with the other. Niemeyer here manages to square his political and architectural convictions in one masterstroke. Devised by Jean Prouvé, the massive curtain wall affirms a desire for transparency, while the large underground hall betrays a more hermetic approach. Between what is said and what is left unsaid, the dialectic of the architect still shines through.

major works

1952 **UN Headquarters (collective),** New York, United States ❀ Numerous projects between 1960 and 2002, Brasilia, Brazil ❀ **1966** **Pestana Casino Park,** Funchal, Portugal ❀ **1978** **Le Volcan (Cultural Center),** Le Havre, France ❀ **1996** **Contemporary Art Museum,** Niterói, Brazil ❀ **2005** **Auditorium,** São Paulo, Brazil

JEAN NOUVEL

There once ran a long wall of gray stone bordering boulevard Raspail behind which hid a strange mass, half townhouse, half *tempietto*. It was in fact the one-time refuge of the American Center for Students and Artists that had relocated to the other side of the Seine some time between 1980 and 1990.

Replacing the stone, a long glass wall some 26 feet (8 meters)—tall rather than concealing—now reveals, in the midst of a garden, a glass block so transparent that it appears liquid. The poetics of the site—a combination of weft and weave—is such that it forces an emotional response: a space of the undefined, of immateriality, of inexpressible concepts, of sensations, and of nuance. It is an aesthetics of generosity that deploys the lines it derives from, rather than a structure. Nouvel has always wanted those who use and visit the buildings he designs to be able to "read" them from every side. Operating on what one might term the ambiguity of limits, in the Fondation Cartier the architect attains the apogee of materialization-dematerialization, managing, by means of structures that are nothing if not minimal, to arouse a maximum of sensation and emotion.

major works

1987 **Institut du Monde Arabe,** Paris, France ❖ 1987 **Nemausus (apartments),** Nîmes, France ❖ 1998 **Dentsu Building,** Tokyo, Japan ❖ 1999 **Culture and congress center,** Lucerne, Switzerland ❖ 2006 **musée du quai Branly,** Paris, France ❖ 2007 **Guthrie Theater,** Minneapolis, United States ❖

DOMINIQUE PERRAULT

The black of the asphalt, the red of the track, the green of the scenery: through them all streaks a white fault line. A fault, a slit, a furrow that plunges down a gentle slope to a depth of 20 meters before climbing out the other side up a broad stairway, reminding one irresistibly of Courbet's *Origin of the World*.

At first, our retinal sensations cannot gauge the size of this faultline, which is only fully appreciable once inside: gigantic, outsized, yet it barely scars the earth. To each side an immense glazed wall the ridge of which, though perfectly orthogonal, seems to curve in a striking effect. The metal fitments set round this mass of glass evoke music paper inscribed with strange, leaping scansions, while the cap nuts screwing them down stand for the endless vibrato of an appoggiatura. Housing 22,000 students in its 75,350 square feet (7000 square meters), flights of stairs strike out inside into the space, ballast that forestalls any latent sense of vertigo. Then follow five floors: classrooms, amphitheaters, auditoriums, gymnasiums, stores, meeting areas, walkways, crossroads, footbridges. As night falls, the fault line is suddenly illuminated and transforms into a gigantic comet of light and color.

A sort of proclamation of "non-architecture" and a perfect illustration of a strategy of concealment, Ewha Women's University is also perhaps where geography takes its revenge on history.

major works
1990 Hôtel Industriel Berlier, Paris, France ✸ **1996 Bibliothèque Nationale de France François-Mitterrand,** Paris, France ✸ **1999 Velodrome,** Berlin, Germany ✸ **2000 Aplix factory,** Nantes, France ✸ **2008 European Court of Justice,** Luxembourg ✸ **2009 Olympic tennis center,** Madrid, Spain

RENZO PIANO

In the center of a peninsula, on the road out of the capital of New Caledonia, perched on a ridge overlooking the ocean and the lagoon, stands a row of eleven boxes arranged as a traditional Kanak village. Blades of iroko wood comprise the structure of these boxes, the tallest of which rises 89 feet (27 meters).

A kind of giant organ comprised of a stand of column-like pines through which the wind whistles, vibrates, sings, creates flowing waves. As the sun sets all ablaze, as is common here, these great pipes suddenly enter a new dimension, displaying all the elegance, measure, and adroitness of the architect, combined with an acknowledged respect for local topography and culture.

Nonetheless, the Centre Culturel Tjibaou is much more than the vernacular architecture of New Caledonia updated and upscaled. In Nouméa, Piano has produced a prototype for green architecture, a manifesto of low-tech after his high-tech performance at the Centre Pompidou co-signed with Richard Rogers twenty years previously.

And, beyond the technical aspect, beyond even the sheer quality of the design, his architecture is infused with real cultural and political significance.

major works
1977 **Centre Pompidou** (with Richard Rogers), Paris, France ❈ 1986 **Menil Collection,** Houston, United States ❈ 1990 **San Nicola Stadium,** Bari, Italy ❈ 1994 **Kansai Airport,** Osaka, Japan ❈ 2001 **Maison Hermès,** Tokyo, Japan ❈ 2006 **Extension of the Morgan Library,** New York, United States

CHRISTIAN DE PORTZAMPARC

On the unprepossessing plateau of Kirchberg, the Philharmonie performs a flamboyantly baroque spectacle where the ellipse is king: ringed by a forest of pillars, the slightly distorted oval shapes into something resembling a filter that shows the way through the looking glass.

Once on the other side of this filter, one reaches a galleried foyer whose folds form a kind of second facade, like a cliff slashed with great vertical fault lines that change in hue, while the ramps, bridges, and staircases seem to roll along ad infinitum; there then comes the great auditorium, a vast hall whose walls are delineated, divided up in such a fashion as to appear articulated by autonomous towers with, once again, impressive effects of lighting, color, and diffraction. But the apotheosis is surely attained in the chamber music room: a Möbius strip reinterpreted as a leaf that is unfurled, twisted, flattened, and remounted in an endless cycle until at last, in a single bound, it blends into the great ellipse. Quite apart from once again recalling his special relationship with music, Portzamparc's Luxembourg Philharmonie exemplifies his architectural standpoint: a poetic yet rigorous system of combinations involving memory and innocence, history and exploration, fragmentation and clarity.

major works

1979 Les Hautes-Formes (high-rise apartments), Paris, France ✦ **1995** Cité de la Musique, Paris, France ✦ **1995** Crédit Lyonnais Tower, Lille, France ✦ **2003** Dior Building, New York, United States ✦ **2004** French Embassy, Berlin, Germany ✦ **2009** Cidade de la Música, Rio de Janeiro, Brazil

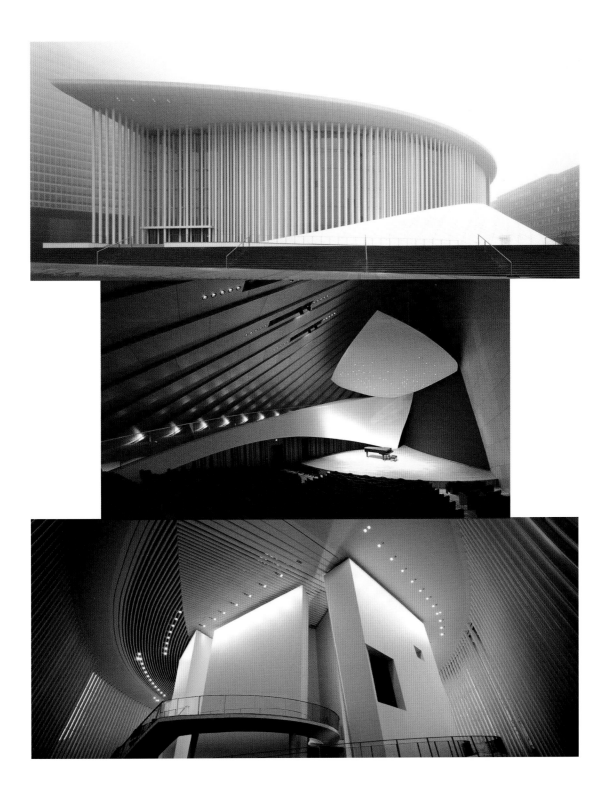

RUDY RICCIOTTI

Before it was even on the drawing board, on announcing where the site would be, Ricciotti insisted: "The project will have to exist through the retention of matter. It will have only skin and bones." Except that here, the architect reverses the customary roles: the bones, a load-bearing structure comprised of canted black concrete pillars, enclose a skin consisting of a glass curtain wall extending over the entire height of this massive, 115 foot (35 meter) long by 59 foot (18 meter) wide building that rises to a height of 85 feet (26 meters). The role played by light is inverted, too: in the day, it pours into the building in great gulps; by night, it is the building itself that emits it, like an oil lamp or lighthouse. The topsy-turvy game continues: like an open fortress, both lightweight and dense, the sleek concrete and glass allow marks, scratches, and scars to remain visible.

Evocative of violence and passion, of cruelty and intransigence, of impurity and indetermination, the Pavillon Noir (Black Flag) is a name that fits this radical monument like a glove. Ricciotti has a reputation for taste and his masterly and polemical rhetoric, both of which transpire in his structures by means of a root-and-branch aesthetics that puts him firmly in camp of the informal, the irregular, the irreverent, those who tackle the question of architecture with vehemence coupled with skill and precision.

major works
1994 **Stadium,** Vitrolles, France ✵ 1995 **Naval Base,** Bandol, France ✵ 1999 **Concert Hall,** Potsdam, Germany ✵ 2000 **Peace Bridge,** Seoul, South Korea ✵ 2008 **Université Paris VII Denis-Diderot,** Paris, France

RICHARD ROGERS

London, like all the great capitals of the world, made a huge effort to celebrate the new millennium in 2000. Among the events marking the occasion, one was to gain particular notoriety.

Astride the Greenwich meridian, on a loop in the Thames, and facing Westminster, the dawn of the millennium saw the erection of a gigantic structure, an immense stretch of canvas of some 1,076,000 square feet (100,000 square meters), coated with a white, semi-opaque, semi-crystalline thermoplastic polymer. A thin, stretched cloth unfurling over an incredible network of cables bolted to 12 great masts, each towering to 100 meters.

This tour de force was signed Richard Rogers who, to spice the Dome up still further, handed over the interior design to Zaha Hadid, an Iraqi-British architect who was beginning to make a name for herself. It was she who fitted out the vast space for the diverse technological attractions filling it, material evidence of the leap into the twenty-first century, which was to be visited by more than six million people during the year before it shut, only to reopen for other leisure activities.

With his iconic Millennium Dome, Rogers once again showed his savoir faire and taste for total legibility in a construction that is treated as a powerful machine of lightness and transparency, integrating perfectly with the public arena.

major works
1977 Centre Pompidou (with Renzo Piano), Paris, France ❂ **1986 Lloyd's Building,** London, United Kingdom ❂ **1998 Palais de Justice** (law courts), Bordeaux, France ❂ **2005 Barajas Airport,** Madrid, Spain ❂ **2005 National Assembly for Wales,** Cardiff, United Kingdom ❂ **2006 Neptune's Way Bridge,** Glasgow, United Kingdom

r&sie

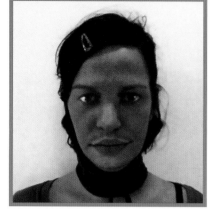

A crashing wave of asphalt, a gentle black hillock echoing the green foothills around it. On the road into the small town of Tokamashi, a twenty-space public parking lot of 984 square feet (300 square meters) of unusual, even disturbing form that exposes entrails containing an open-air space: the Art Front Gallery 590 square feet (180 square meters). A fusion of the arts and the car: an odd place for a meeting. R8Sie (a contraction of Roche and Stéphanie that is read "*hérésie*"; i.e. "heresy"), is above all the tandem of François Roche and Stéphanie Lavaux. But the agency is a movable feast and many young architects have cut their teeth in their team. More than just an architectural practice, R8Sie functions more like a research lab. Experimentation, exploration, evolution, and mutation are the keywords in its business. "R8Sie is primarily an enterprise that concocts heterotopic, paranoiac contraptions, vectors or bearers of narratives that can be understood only by those who take the risk of following it, of following them," François Roche declares.

R8Sie, for whom or which architecture is a mutant organism, has no end of epigones; probably because it encapsulates the thousand-year-old tradition of utopia, independence, autonomy, identity, and difference so well.

major projects and works

2001 Barak House, Sommières, France ✹ **2002 (Un)Plug,** Project for a tower at La Défense, France ✹ **2002 Project for a contemporary art museum** (winning entry for a competition), Bangkok, Thailand ✹ **2003 Hybrid Muscle,** Eco-village project in collaboration with Philippe Parreno, Chiang Mai, Thailand ✹ **2005 Plans for the museum of glaciology,** Evolène, Switzerland ✹ **2008 I'm Lost in Paris, Lab house,** Paris, France

SANAA

In all the architectural projects of the SANAA tandem (formed of Kazuo Sejima and Ryue Nishizawa) the desire for sobriety in expression and use of space is explicit, as if they reject and eschew mass in a poetics of situation which, though in an absolutely contemporary idiom, corresponds in every point to the time-honored Japanese tradition of the lightweight and the simple. But these qualities are counterbalanced by incredible complexity, creating cozy structures, modest, yet nonetheless sociable.

With the New Museum of Contemporary Art in New York, inaugurated in 2007 in the Bowery, a district long left for dead and only now being revived, SANAA pursues this path of the abstract, the immaterial, the intangible.

The eccentrically arranged stacks of six rectangular boxes certainly form a dramatic and dynamic composition on the Manhattan skyline, but, wrapped in aluminum mesh, they also convey a fragile translucence. An elaborate, light-permeable membrane, a papery skin that shifts and vibrates. From the outside, all appears smooth, enclosed, impregnable. Once entered, the space of the museum shows just how porous its skin is, and how the light floods through all the vast, adaptable display areas, all entirely independent and each of a different height.

Everything seems to float, structures disappear, one slides rather than walks, and the eye is left free to revel in the art.

major works
1997 **N Museum,** Wakayama, Japan ❁ 1998 **Residential block,** Motosu, Japan ❁ 1999 **O Museum,** Nagano, Japan ❁ 2003 **Dior Building,** Tokyo, Japan ❁ 2004 **21st Century Museum of Contemporary Art,** Kanazawa, Japan ❁ 2005 **Zollverein School for Management and Design,** Essen, Germany

JOSEP LLUÍS SERT

A haven, an apologia for *la dolce vita*. Charles Baudelaire's famous line "*luxe, calme et volupté*" is here more than apt. Nestling in waves of sweet-smelling greenery, the Fondation Maeght by Josep Lluis Sert, that preeminently "Mediterranean" architect, is an absolute miniature masterpiece.

In Saint-Paul-de-Vence, Sert testifies to the fact that modernist sobriety, something he has always espoused, excludes neither imagination nor invention. As if placed on some giant chessboard, the reception space, art and exhibition center, library, chapel, and house (for the exclusive use of artistic and literary friends) seamlessly succeed one another. A place studded with any number of patios—the Giacometti court, the Miró maze, the Braque pool, the Bury fountain, and others, and, last but not least, the majestic umbrella pines. The gardens, dotted with sculptures by artists close to the Maeght family, enter into a rewarding dialogue with the local stone, brick, and concrete, the trilogy of materials Sert used in the construction of the museum. Inside, thanks to a system employing reinforced-concrete half-vaults, daylight floods the galleries.

The domestication of light, the omnipresence of water, the circulation of air and natural ventilation, all perfectly adapted to the exceptional conditions of the Provence climate, all make the Fondation Maeght a genuine precursor of "green" architecture, of optimum environmental quality.

> Là, tout n'est qu'ordre et beauté,
> Luxe, calme et volupté

Baudelaire's lines course through this *invitation to the voyage*. And whoever has not been lucky enough to attend at least one evening concert at the Fondation Maeght has missed a glorious instance of *la dolce vita*.

major works

1937 Spanish Republic Pavilion, International Exposition, Paris, France ✦ **1965 Holyoke Center,** Harvard University, Cambridge, United States ✦ **1965 Boston University Campus,** Boston, United States ✦ **1973 Harvard Science Center,** Cambridge, United States ✦ **1975 Fondació Joan Miró,** Barcelona, Spain ✦ **1976 Eastwood and Westwood Apartments/Roosevelt Island,** New York, United States

BERNARD TSCHUMI

Architecture Faculty
Florida International University
Miami, United States
2003

In Miami, Bernard Tschumi strives to set the scene and arrange a space for the threefold revolution in information science, interdisciplinarity, and ideology that has shaken the foundations of architectural teaching, in total contradiction with the fine art tradition. The space, though far from the heart of the city, is thus conceived of as a mobile entity at equal distance—as virtual culture demands—from New York, Paris, Tokyo, London, Delhi, and Beijing. The core of the building is left open to the air, a vast common space, at once cohesive and productive. A social and cultural space toward which converge the many fluxes of the school so that, whatever its population density, the students responsible for the life and dynamism of the place can keep in constant movement.

In keeping with the architect's conception, we have here junction and disjunction: movement, action, and space. The result is a symphony of walkways, footbridges, railings, and passages casting shadows over the buildings, imbuing them with life, creating vibration and motion.

And then there is the use, unusual in the United States, of colored ceramics, a tribute in yellow, orange, and red paid to Florida's Latino culture. Like gentle music wafting in the sun, the Florida International University campus is intended to cater to the 25,000 students and carry them away to other, more distant horizons: the enameled gardens of Samarkand or Isfahan, the Alcazar of Seville, or the Alhambra of Granada.

major works
1984–95 **Parc de la Villette,** Paris, France ✸ 1997 **Le Fresnoy, Studio National des Arts Contemporains,** Tourcoing, France ✸ 1998 **The Lerner Student Center, Columbia University,** New York, United States ✸ 2001 **Vacheron Constantin headquarters and factory,** Geneva, Switzerland ✸ 2008 **Athletic center, University of Cincinnati,** United States ✸ 2009 **Acropolis Museum,** Athens, Greece

MINORU YAMASAKI

Is there no escape?

"These towers were such abstract, such dizzying buildings that their dimensions had no connection with those of the city. It was no longer possible to tell if four hundred meters was really very different from six or eight hundred meters. Beyond a certain height, the impact on the environment is the same and comparisons are odious; while the skyline looks very different. These towers, these feats of engineering that had transformed Manhattan, seemed curiously to have fallen from the sky. They were beyond words, and neither yesterday nor today has anyone any real notion of just how much effort was expended in designing and building them.

They were not integrated as twin towers; they were experienced as a whole, a living unit that appeared to symbolize the grandeur of Manhattan," the architect Christian de Portzamparc, the first French winner of the Pritzker Prize in 1994, informed his friend the French writer Philippe Sollers in their joint work *Voir-Écrire* (Calmann-Lévy). A symbol of Manhattan, the Twin Towers were designed and built by the American architect of Japanese descent Minoru Yamasaki, who, in the 1930s, had been close to another symbol of Manhattan with Shreve, Lamb and Harmon, the architects behind the Empire State Building (1931).

Yamasaki's career was somewhat atypical. His first notable and austerely modernistic project was the Pruitt Igoe housing project, built in St. Louis, Missouri in 1955, and demolished in 1975 due to its notorious unpopularity. By an architect who, in spite of a tireless search for elegance, espoused a hesitant, multi-faceted eclecticism, the World Trade Center was Yamasaki's magnum opus, and parts of its vocabulary recur in the Torre Picasso later erected in Madrid.

But in New York, at 8:46 a.m. on that September 11, 2001, a Boeing 767, American Airlines Flight 11, struck the North Tower; and then, at 9:03 a.m., another Boeing 767, this time United Airlines Flight 175, plowed into the South Tower. The Twin Towers of the World Trade Center, that great symbol of American economic power, were dead; as if the myth, the curse of Babel, had come back to haunt us.

APPENDIXES

A SHORT GUIDE TO STYLES

There was Babylon and the ziggurat, a stepped religious building, a magic spiral linking heaven and earth that inspired the myth of the Tower of Babel. Then there was Egypt whose mysterious cenotaphs Michel de Broin, an eminent scholar, described as: "a stone heap in the shape of a pyramid with, in the middle, a mystery." Adding with a smile: "The Greeks kept the mystery and set up columns around it." Let us, then, start with the Greeks.

ABOVE
Diller, Scofidio,
Renfro, Institute
of Contemporary Art
Boston, United States,
2006.

GREEK ARCHITECTURE

An illustration of the triumph of reason, the temple is the embodiment of Greek architecture: reason given material form by the simple juxtaposition of horizontal elements (the ground and stone lintels bearing a double-pitch roof) and vertical elements (posts or columns). Three orders were to follow from the sixth to the fourth centuries BCE. Of supreme simplicity, the Doric order superimposes the base of the temple, the column, and the capital, almost without decoration. The Doric is characteristic of mainland Greece, as in the Parthenon. The Ionic order developed in the islands and Asia Minor. Characteristic of the refined if ostentatious taste of the local population, it opposes the rawness of the Doric with a concern for elegance: the result is slenderer columns that are placed on the base in a more subtle manner, with the capital enriched with two scrolls, or volutes. The Ionic order perpetuates the orthogonality, rigor, and rationality of the Doric, but renders it considerably more supple. Its successor, the Corinthian order, developed into a stylistic and formal language that was refined and ostentatious. This order is characterized by a capital whose scrolls are wrapped in acanthus leaves.

Ictinus and Callicrates, The Parthenon, Athens, Greece, 447–422 BCE.

ROMAN ARCHITECTURE

The Pantheon, Rome, Italy, 125 CE.

If the Romans borrowed from the Greeks, they also introduced notable differences. In particular they superimposed the three orders (the Doric on the lowest level and the Corinthian on the highest), introduced the wholesale use of brick (with the facades clad in marble or faced with stone), and, in the majority of their buildings, made use of arches. In addition, the Romans "democratized" architecture and, no longer the preserve of temples and palaces, the art appeared in public buildings (triumphal arches, amphitheaters, basilicas, thermal baths) and in other sizable constructions (aqueducts, viaducts). Buildings with cupolas became almost commonplace, the most famous being the Pantheon in Rome, with its small central oculus through which light pours, flooding the entire space, and which still remains a mysterious tour de force.

ROMANESQUE ARCHITECTURE

At once heir to and continuation of Roman architecture, this period reached its apogee in the twelfth century. Thanks to buttresses used to balance out the resulting thrusts, vaults could span naves with vast surface areas. The barrel vault and semicircular arch are its foremost characteristics. The development of monastic orders (at Cluny and Cîteaux) and the Crusades ensured that it soon became widespread throughout Europe and the Middle East. Succeeding decades witnessed its unfettered originality, in particular as regards the composition of church portals, the design of facades, and external ornamentation. Inspired both by Rome and Byzantium, but unafraid of asserting its own language, a decorative art developed comprising strange figures, fantastic animals, and unknown plants, and not unconnected to fears of imminent apocalypse. This was a time when church fronts became veritable "books of stone," which spread the lessons of the New Testament to an illiterate populace, a period in which castles, once made out of wood, were reinforced and built in stone.

Sénanque Abbey, Gordes, France, 1148–1240.

GOTHIC ARCHITECTURE

The Gothic originated in research, technical developments, knowledge of physical phenomena, solutions to the problems of statics, and, ultimately, from a tireless quest for light. In short, this meant opening walls and raising them as high as possible, in an attempt to recreate the bond between the earth and the heavens. Born in the Île-de-France on the banks of the Seine before rapidly spreading north (England) and east (Germany), Gothic architecture represents a structural revolution that was to attain its stylistic acme in the thirteenth century in the form of the Flamboyant style, whose most moving testimony is the Sainte-Chapelle in Paris. An architecture of curves and tensions, of flame and light, of tracery and color, it displays dazzling virtuosity.

Pierre de Montreuil or Jean de Chelles, Sainte-Chapelle, Paris, France, 1248.

RENAISSANCE ARCHITECTURE

Florence was the most important court in Italy and it was here that the Renaissance was adopted and codified. To do away with the Romanesque and Gothic styles and embrace the ancient world, all the while exploiting and improving technical innovations: such was the ambition of Renaissance architects. This project was greatly assisted by the discovery of perspective and developments in geometry. It was in this period that the architect as we know him today was born: an autonomous artist, with his own, individual sensitivity and specific talents. Brunelleschi and Alberti were the leading lights. The former with the striking and unparalleled dome of the cathedral of Santa Maria dei Fiore in Florence, while Alberti imposed the chief characteristics of antiquity: bases, pediments, pilasters, and columns.

Andrea Palladio, Villa Almenico-Capra (known as La Rotonda) Vicenza, Italy, 1570.

The process was marked by a preoccupation with proportion, symmetry, and regularity. Bramante, Michelangelo, Leonardo da Vinci, and the Sangallos in Italy, and Salomon de Brosse, Philibert Delorme, Jacques Androuet du Cerceau, and Pierre Lescot in France were its main sixteenth-century exponents. Extending beyond historically important buildings (places of worship, palaces), Renaissance architects designed a number of public sites and patrician villas, and treated the urban space as a single unit, thus anticipating town planning. Pushing aesthetics, harmony, beauty, and decoration to their utmost, the architecture of the Renaissance developed into mannerism, the finest example of which is Palladio's La Rotonda near Vicenza.

BAROQUE ARCHITECTURE

Back to Rome, where the period was a strange one. An era when—in the wake of Galileo and Kepler, Spinoza in philosophy, Rembrandt in painting, and Leibniz and Newton in mathematics—people tried to apprehend the infinite, to track its trajectory, and understand its value. As regards architecture, it was the trio of Bernini, Borromini, and Pietro da Cortona who pushed back the limits, devising in the process countless variations on the theme of the oval: a shape that, thanks to spiraling or oscillating effects, permits infinite spatial combinations, unlike the square and circle, perfect forms that had so delighted the Renaissance.

The greatest lesson of baroque architecture is surely that it treats the city as a stage. The city as backdrop, the urban fabric as theater, in an interplay between wave and ellipse, between voluptuous ecstasy and intellectual ambiguity. An art of presence, of the instant, of exaltation, of physical intensity, of love and death, the baroque invaded Germany, Austria, Bohemia, Poland, as well as Spain, Portugal (of Portuguese origin, the word *barroco* means "irregular pearl"), and Latin America, but its influence was slight in France, too measured and classical to yield to such paroxysms.

Dominikus Zimmermann, Wieskirche, Steingaden, Germany, 1745–54.

FRENCH CLASSICISM

Yet another return to the classical. Nourished on the harmonious proportions of antiquity, French classical architecture aimed first and foremost to impose the power and prosperity of the kingdom under Louis XIV. Concerned with glorifying the king through harmony, equilibrium, and symmetry, it was centered on order and reason, with pared-down decorative effects counterbalanced by generous volumes. Noble and simple lines, in reaction to the tumult and outpourings of the baroque. Prior to classicism proper, one might cite the Place des Vosges in Paris, initiated by Henri IV and completed by Louis XIII, as a perfect example of logic, utility, and simplicity. Later, by pushing the preoccupation with order and harmony still further, French classicism concerned itself with the city, striving to solve questions such as hygiene and congestion. Utopia was reborn, reaching its apogee in the many projects and occasional works of what it has become customary to call "revolutionary architects": Boullée, Lequeu, and Ledoux, and in particular at the royal saltworks, the Saline Royale d'Arc-and-Senans by the last named.

Louis Le Vau (for the classical-style areas 1661–70), Château de Versailles, Versailles, France, 1623–1783.

ECLECTICISMS

Each period generates "offshoots" that extrapolate or backtrack, that tone down or exaggerate. Thus from baroque was born—chiefly in Germany and Central Europe—rococo, which relies on asymmetrical curves or counter-curves and exuberant arabesques. Another outgrowth was rocaille, the only genuine French concession, if a delicate and understated one, to the baroque. Later, in the nineteenth century, at the time when the Middle Ages were being rediscovered, Gothic Revival made an entrance that was all-conquering in England, but which throughout Europe was to give rise to an unbridled and sometimes fiddly romantic style. In France, Viollet-le-Duc, with the

Charles Garnier, Opéra, Paris, France, 1861–75.

restoration and reconstitution of Notre-Dame de Paris and the Château de Pierrefonds, was a key figure, although he went far beyond mere romanticism, in particular as regards his use of new techniques and materials (steel) that heralded the onset of industrial architecture. Still in France, Charles Garnier, with the Opéra in Paris which conflates the influence of Pompeii, of St. Peter's in Rome, and of Versailles, gives free rein to eclecticism and has no fear of overload or nationalist tub-thumping.

ART NOUVEAU

On the eve of the twentieth century, the West was rediscovering and taking inspiration from nature. One such tribute was art nouveau, known variously depending on the country as Modern Style in England, as Jugendstil in Germany, Sezessionstil in Austria, Nieuwe Kunst in the Netherlands, Stile Liberty in Italy, Tiffany Style in the United States, Modernismo in Spain, and in France as art nouveau—or, more derisively, as *style nouille* ("noodle [including the sense of "silly"] style"). It encompassed many arts and crafts: painting, graphic arts, jewelry, furniture. In architecture, it marked the triumph of the curved line, of natural and plant-like forms, which did not necessarily exclude the recourse to rigorous geometry.

The architects of art nouveau privileged no particular material, blithely combining stone, brick, wood, iron, steel, and glass. Their ideal was fusion, every kind of fusion, between nature and culture, as well as between structure and decoration. All resolutely independent and autonomous, the leading lights in art nouveau were the Frenchman Hector Guimard, the creator inter alia of the famous metro entrances in Paris; the Belgian Victor Horta, whose elegance and lightness were described as the "whiplash style"; the Catalan Antoni Gaudi whose Sagrada Familia in Barcelona remains unfinished to this day;

and the Austrian Otto Wagner whose Postsparkasse (Post Office Savings Bank) in Vienna is a pure masterpiece.

Antoni Gaudi, Sagrada Familia (unfinished), Barcelona, Spain, 1884–26.

ART DECO

This was yet another reaction, one that was to mark the years 1920–30 and which owes its name to the International Exhibition of Modern Decorative and Industrial Arts in Paris in 1925. Once again, techniques and materials (and in particular reinforced concrete that could be cast in any form) fostered a new means of expression, a new architectural language. In architecture, the twin raison d'être of this movement, which found its expression in various domains, was to simplify and to democratize. Architects turned their hand to

William van Alen, Chrysler Building, New York, United States, 1928–30.

projects, plans, and inventions for the world to come with greater rigor and simplicity than in other areas of expression. The results tended to be closer to cubism than fauvism and follow the "avant-gardes of the twentieth century" that came into being shortly after the First World War: De Stijl (1917) in the Netherlands, the Bauhaus (1919) in Germany, Vhutemas (1920) in the Soviet Union, and Esprit Nouveau (1920) in France were all harbingers of future modernist movements.

GLOSSARY OF KEY ARCHITECTURE TERMS

A

Architecture

The definition given in the dictionary is brief and to the point: "The art of designing and executing built structures and spaces."

The word "art" is important in that it distinguishes architecture clearly from building and construction. In other words, the priority is given to the idea, concept, expression, or style, over the techniques and materials, without of course ignoring the latter. But the techniques and materials are only the means, helpmates in the service of something else far more vast and complex. Already, in the first century CE, in his treatise *De Architectura*, the Roman Vitruvius wrote: "Architecture is a science covering a wide range of study and knowledge. The fruit of practice and theory, it can embrace and judge all the productions of the other arts." And he insists on what he calls the triad of beauty, solidity, and utility (suitability). In the modern era, Le Corbusier provides another enlightening definition: "The masterly, correct and magnificent play of volumes brought together in light." Today architecture is entering a phase during which the demands, needs, and tools with which it is concerned are undergoing wholesale change, thereby extending still further the scope of its competence, the complexity of its practices, and the diversity of its forms of expression.

Architect

A standard definition would run: "The architect is a professional whose function is to design and direct the realization of a piece of architecture for the entity commissioning him or her, which can be a private individual, a company, or a public body. In many countries, he or she has to be licensed and insured, since they remain professionally liable for a number of years depending on the country concerned. An 'architect' can be an individual or a legal entity (an architectural practice or agency)." Such a definition, of course, hardly accounts for the complexity of the role and the practice of an architect who in turn and simultaneously has to be an artist, a technician, and a manager. Hence it is scarcely surprising that in tandem with their architectural studies, numerous future practitioners combine other disciplines, such as town planning, heritage studies, engineering, ecology, landscaping, etc.

Atrium

A covered version, today generally constructed with glass, of the ancient *patio*.

Attic

Technically, a small additional floor often used to conceal the roof.

B

Bond

A particular way of laying and arranging bricks (and occasionally stonework) for structural and/or decorative purposes.

C

Cantilever

An overhanging part of construction supported by counterweight.

Capital

That part of a column standing at the junction of the support and the load.

Client

The entity that places the order or commission, be it a private individual, a company, or a public body, often the owner of the resulting construction.

Colonnade

A row of columns.

Curtain wall

Generally in glass and/or metal, a non-load-bearing wall whose function is to screen off or protect the interior of the building.

E

Elevation

External or interior facade of a construction; a drawing showing this.

F

Footprint

The surface area occupied by a building and its amenities (not including roadways).

P

Pediment

Crown of a building above the facade, generally triangular in form. Now in danger of extinction, except among advocates of postmodernism.

Peristyle

Colonnade in front of a building's facade. The hypostyle is an enclosed interior space with a ceiling borne on columns.

Pilotis

Pilotis have been employed from time immemorial. These vertical supports liberate the construction from the ground and are both protective and insulating. Le Corbusier made them a modern architectural "must-have."

Project

Etymologically, the word project means "to throw something forward," meaning that it is produced prior to something else. Its definition can be understood in two ways: as the preparation, conception, and development of a construction that is actually built; or else, a vision or idea for some future time. As regards architecture, and however the term is understood, the point is not to be afraid of it, but to decipher it, for architects work on projects all day and every day. For them, the vaguest dream, a stab in the dark, a freehand sketch, a preparatory drawing, a losing entry for a competition or unsuccessful commission, a realization—all can be called a *project*. The stress then is on the fact that the project, the subject, that is, the idea, the concept even, takes precedence over the object.

S

Schedule

Upstream of the project, the schedule or program is a document handed over to the architect featuring all the information and specifications (location, type, requirements, functions, budget) necessary for the development of the project (plan). In the immense majority of cases, this bulky document (running to several hundred pages) is dedicated to the conditions and works envisaged rather than the architectural plan: a list of the building's requisite characteristics, with little space for intention and that concentrates on the "how" rather than the "what" or "why." As if the architect's job—already multifarious and complex enough—included contracting out the construction.

Shoebox (style)

Pejorative term designating low-rises or high-rises ("rabbit hutches"), extended to any residential construction showing a manifest want of architectural foresight.

Site

At once territory, topography, milieu, context, terrain, orientation, climate, history, memory, constraint, and rule book. These the architect has to juggle and choose whether to blend in, confront, counterbalance, undermine, etc.

Skin

The time of walls and facades in the strict sense is passed. These are being increasingly replaced by shells and membranes, the result of spectacular advances in technology. These breathing, translucent, flexible, vibratile skins are more like envelopes than enclosures and often amount to veritable little eco-factories. They often resemble bubbles, dragonfly wings, clouds, and so on.

T

Town planning

Town planning is a vast domain since it covers the regional development of urban centers. That is to say, it is simultaneously a science and a practice, in which politics and geography, economics and sociology, the social sciences and ecology all have a part to play. Studies of the urban phenomenon and the organization of the metropolis are instrumental in planning for pedestrian flow, housing, road networks and highways, amenity zones, public transport, etc.

THE PRIZEWINNERS

Three prizes, two wholeheartedly international, the third European, are hugely coveted by architects, as the juries' selection tends to be consistent and because they offer fame and fortune and open all doors. To be awarded one of these prizes—or several even—means that one's future is assured. They are listed below in chronological order—which is also, coincidentally, their order of importance.

THE PRITZKER PRIZE

Founded in 1979 by Jay A. Pritzker, the man behind Hyatt Hotels, it is worth 100,000 US dollars and is regarded as the Nobel Prize for architecture.

1979 ∘ Philip Johnson (United States)
1980 ∘ Luis Barragán (Mexico)
1981 ∘ James Stirling (United Kingdom)
1982 ∘ Kevin Roche (United States)
1983 ∘ Ieoh Ming Pei (United States)
1984 ∘ Richard Meier (United States)
1985 ∘ Hans Hollein (Austria)
1986 ∘ Gottfried Böhm (Germany)
1987 ∘ Kenzo Tange (Japan)
1988 ∘ Gordon Bunshaft (United States) and Oscar Niemeyer (Brazil)
1989 ∘ Frank O. Gehry (United States)
1990 ∘ Aldo Rossi (Italy)
1991 ∘ Robert Venturi (United States)
1992 ∘ Álvaro Siza (Portugal)
1993 ∘ Fumihiko Maki (Japan)
1994 ∘ Christian de Portzamparc (France)
1995 ∘ Tadao Ando (Japan)
1996 ∘ Rafael Moneo (Spain)
1997 ∘ Sverre Fehn (Norway)
1998 ∘ Renzo Piano (Italy)
1999 ∘ Norman Foster (United Kingdom)
2000 ∘ Rem Koolhaas (Netherlands)
2001 ∘ Jacques Herzog and Pierre de Meuron (Switzerland)
2002 ∘ Glenn Murcutt (Australia)
2003 ∘ Jørn Utzon (Denmark)
2004 ∘ Zaha Hadid (United Kingdom)
2005 ∘ Thom Mayne (United States)
2006 ∘ Paolo Mendes da Rocha (Brazil)
2007 ∘ Richard Rogers (United Kingdom)
2008 ∘ Jean Nouvel (France)
2009 ∘ Peter Zumthor (Switzerland)

THE PRAEMIUM IMPERIALE

The Praemium Imperiale, founded in 1988 by the Japan Art Association on the occasion of its centenary, gives a prize of 15 million yen in each of the five disciplines for which it is awarded (painting, sculpture, architecture, music, and theater or cinema).

1989 ∘ Ieoh Ming Pei (United States)
1990 ∘ James Stirling (United Kingdom)
1991 ∘ Gae Aulenti (Italy)
1992 ∘ Frank O. Gehry (United States)
1993 ∘ Kenzo Tange (Japan)
1994 ∘ Charles Correa (India)
1995 ∘ Renzo Piano (Italy)

1996 ∘ Tadao Ando (Japan)
1997 ∘ Richard Meier (United States)
1998 ∘ Álvaro Siza (Portugal)
1999 ∘ Fumihiko Maki (Japan)
2000 ∘ Richard Rogers (United Kingdom)
2001 ∘ Jean Nouvel (France)
2002 ∘ Norman Foster (United Kingdom)
2003 ∘ Rem Koolhaas (Netherlands)
2004 ∘ Oscar Niemeyer (Brazil)
2005 ∘ Yoshio Taniguchi (Japan)
2006 ∘ Frei Otto (Germany)
2007 ∘ Jacques Herzog and Pierre de Meuron (Switzerland)
2008 ∘ Peter Zumthor (Switzerland)

THE MIES VAN DER ROHE PRIZE

Founded in 1988, jointly by the Fundació Mies van der Rohe in Barcelona and the European Commission, the European Union Prize for Contemporary Architecture Mies van der Rohe Award boasts an envelope of 60,000 euros and is awarded every two years. Entrants are limited to the twenty-seven European Union nations, together with Croatia, Iceland, Liechtenstein, Macedonia, Norway, Serbia, and Turkey.

1988 ∘ Álvaro Siza (Portugal)
1990 ∘ Norman Foster (United Kingdom)
1992 ∘ Esteve Bonell and Francesc Rius (Spain)
1994 ∘ Nicholas Grimshaw (United Kingdom)
1997 ∘ Dominique Perrault (France)
1999 ∘ Peter Zumthor (Switzerland)
2001 ∘ Rafael Moneo (Spain)
2003 ∘ Zaha Hadid (United Kingdom)
2005 ∘ Rem Koolhaas (Netherlands)
2007 ∘ Luis Mansilla and Emilio Tuñón (Spain)
2009 ∘ Snøhetta (Norway)

The accumulation of prizes is a curious alchemical process resulting from a blend of talent and a steady hand, innovation and competence, intellectual ability and visual expressiveness, sociability and worldliness. Two entrants have been awarded both the Pritzker and the Mies van der Rohe prizes: Zaha Hadid (the only woman to appear in these lists) and Rafael Moneo; twelve have won the Pritzker and the Praemium Imperiale: Frank O. Gehry, Richard Meier, Ieoh Ming Pei, Oscar Niemeyer, Richard Rogers, James Stirling, Jean Nouvel, Renzo Piano, Tadao Ando, Fumihiko Maki, Kenzo Tange, and Herzog & de Meuron; only four have netted all three prizes: Norman Foster, Rem Koolhaas, Álvaro Siza, and Peter Zumthor.

WHERE TO SEE ARCHITECTURE

BRAZIL
Paço Imperial
Praça XV de Novembro, 48
Centro, Rio de Janeiro
Tel: +5521 2215 2622
www.pacoimperial.com.br/

CANADA
**Canadian Centre for Architecture
(CCA)**
1920 rue Baile
Montreal, Quebec
Tel: +1 514 939 7026
www.cca.qc.ca

DENMARK
Dansk Arkitectur Center (DAC)
Strandgade 27B
Copenhagen
Tel: +45 3257 1930
english.dac.dk

FINLAND
Museum of Finnish Architecture
Kasarmikatu 24
Helsinki
Tel: +358 9 8567 5100
www.mfa.fi

FRANCE
**Cité de l'Architecture
et du Patrimoine**
1 place du Trocadéro-et-du-11-
novembre
75016 Paris
Tel: +33 (0)1 58 51 52 00
www.citechaillot.org

Galerie d'Architecture
11 rue des Blancs-Manteaux
75004 Paris
Tel: +33 (0)1 49 96 64 00
www.galerie-architecture.fr

Pavillon de l'Arsenal
21 boulevard Morland
75004 Paris
Tel: +33 (0)1 42 76 33 97
www.pavillon-arsenal.com

GERMANY
Aedes East
Rosenthaler Strasse 40-41
Berlin
Tel: +49 030282 7015
www.aedes-arc.de

Deutsches Architekturmuseum (DAM)
Schaumainkai 43
Frankfurt
Tel: +49 69 212 38844
www.dam-online.de/

GREAT BRITAIN
Architectural Association (AA)
36 Bedford Square
London
Tel: +44 20 7887 4021

**RIBA Gallery (Royal Institute
of British Architects)**
66 Portland Place
London
Tel: +44 20 7580 5533
www.riba.org

ITALY
**MAXXI Museo Nazionale
delle Arti del XXI Secolo**
Via Guido Reni
Rome
www.maxxi.parc.beniculturali.it

Triennale di Milano
Viale Alemagna 6
20121 Milan

JAPAN
Galerie MA
Tokyo
www.toto.co.jp

THE NETHERLANDS
ARCAM
Prins Hendrikkade 600
Amsterdam
Tel: +31 20 620 48 78
www.arcam.nl

Nederlands Architectuurinstitut (NAI)
Museumpark 25
Rotterdam
Tel: +31 10 440 1200
www.nai.nl

NORWAY
**National Museum of Art,
Design & Architecture**
Kristian Augusts gate 23
Oslo
Tel: +47 21 98 20 00
www.nationalmuseum.no

SPAIN
**Centre de Cultura Contemporània
de Barcelona (CCCB)**
Montalegre 5
08001 Barcelona
Tel: +34 93 306 41 00
www.cccb.org

Mies van der Rohe Foundació
Avenida Marquès de Comilles
Montjuïc
Barcelona
Tel: +34 93 423 40 16
www.miesbcn.com

SWITZERLAND
**Schweizerisches Architekturmuseum
(SAM)**
Steinenberg 7
Basel
Tel: +41 61 261 14 13
www.sam-basel.org/

UNITED STATES
A+D
6032 Wilshire Blvd
Los Angeles, CA 90036
+1 323 932 9393
www.aplusd.org/

**The Chicago Athenaeum International
Museum of Architecture and Design**
307 N. Michigan Avenue
Chicago, IL 60601
+1 312 372 1083
www.chi-athenaeum.org

National Building Museum
401 F Street NW
Washington, DC 20001
Tel: + 1 202 272 2448|
www.nbm.org

SELECTED BIBLIOGRAPHY

ARDENNE, PAUL. Rudy Ricciotti. Basel: Birkhauser Verlag, 2004.

BANHAM, REYNER. Age of the Masters, a Personal View of Modern Architecture. New York, Evanston, and San Francisco: Harper and Row, 1975.

BLAKE, PETER. Form Follows Fiasco. New York: Little, Brown & Co., 1978.

BOISSIÈRE, OLIVIER. Trois portraits de l'artiste en architecte: Gehry, Site, Tigerman. Paris: Le Moniteur, 1981.

BOISSIÈRE, OLIVIER. Jean Nouvel. Paris: Terrail, 1999.

BONY, ANNE. L'Architecture moderne. Paris: Larousse, 2006.

DE BURE, GILLES. Jean Nouvel. Paris: Artemis, 1992.

DE BURE, GILLES. Claude Vasconi. Paris: Éditions du Regard, 1995.

DE BURE, GILLES. Christian de Portzamparc. Paris: Terrail, 2003.

DE BURE, GILLES. Dominique Perrault. Bilingual ed. Paris: Terrail, 2004.

DE BURE, GILLES. Bernard Tschumi. Paris: Norma, 2008.

CHASLIN, FRANÇOIS. Les Paris de François Mitterrand. Paris: Éditions Gallimard, 1985.

CHASLIN, FRANÇOIS. Jean Nouvel Critiques. Gollion: Infolio, 2008.

COLQUHOUN, ALAN. Modern Architecture. Oxford: Oxford University Press, 2002.

D'ALFONSO, ERNESTO, AND DANILO SAMSA. L'Architecture, les formes et les styles, de l'Antiquité à nos jours. Paris: Solar Éditions, 2002.

EDELMANN, FRÉDÉRIC. In the Chinese City. 2 vols. Barcelona: Actar, 2008.

FLOUQUET, SOPHIE. L'Architecture contemporaine. Paris: Éditions Scala, 2004.

FRAMPTON, KENNETH. Modern Architecture: A Critical History. 4th rev. ed. London: Thames & Hudson, 2007.

FROMONOT, FRANÇOISE. Glenn Murcutt. Paris: Éditions Gallimard, 2003.

GARDINER, STEPHEN. Introduction to Architecture. London: Chancellor, 1993.

GIEDION, SIEGFRIED. Space, Time, Architecture: The Growth of a New Tradition. 5th rev. and enlarged ed. Cambridge, MA: Harvard University Press, 2008.

GOULET, PATRICE. Jean Nouvel. Paris: Éditions du Regard, 1994.

GOULET, PATRICE. Jacques Hondelatte. Des gratte-ciels dans la tête. Paris: Norma, 2004.

JENCKS, CHARLES. The Language of Post-Modern Architecture. New York: Rizzoli, 1997.

JENCKS, CHARLES. Late-Modern Architecture. New York: Rizzoli, 1980.

JODIDIO, PHILIP. Architecture Now. 6 vols. Cologne: Taschen, 2002–09.

JODIDIO, PHILIP. Houses. Architecture Now. Cologne: Taschen, 2008.

KOOLHAAS, REM. Delirious New York: A Retroactive Manifesto for Manhattan. New York: Monacelli, 1978.

PARENT, CLAUDE. L'Architecte, bouffon social. Paris: Casterman, 1982.

RAMBERT, FRANCIS. Massimiliano Fuksas. Paris: Éditions du Regard, 1997.

RAMBERT, FRANCIS. Architecture Tomorrow. Paris: Terrail, 2005.

RUDOFSKY, BERNARD. Architecture without Architects. Albuquerque: University of New Mexico Press, 1987.

TAFURI, MANFREDO. Theories and History of Architecture. New York: Icon (Harpe), 1981.

TAFURI, MANFREDO. The Sphere and the Labyrinth: Avant-Gardes and Architecture from Piranesi to the 1970's. Cambridge, MA: MIT Press, 1990.

TAFURI, MANFEDO, AND FRANSCESCO DAL CO. Architettura contemporanea. Milan: Electa, 1976.

TRÉTIACK, PHILIPPE. Faut-il pendre les architectes? Paris: Le Seuil, 2001.

TSCHUMI, BERNARD. Architecture and Disjunction. Cambridge, MA: MIT Press, 1996.

WIGLEY, MARK. White Walls— Designer Dresses: The Fashioning of Modern Architecture. Cambridge, MA: MIT Press, 2001.

ZEVI, BRUNO. Architecture as Space: How to Look at Architecture. New York: Da Capo, 1993.

ZEVI, BRUNO. The Modern Language of Architecture. Cambridge, MA and New York: Da Capo Press, 1994.

INDEX
OF PROPER
NAMES

PHOTOGRAPHIC CREDITS

The author would like to take this
opportunity to thank, for their intelligent
assistance: Michel de Broin, Hélène Brom,
and Francis Rambert, as well as
Sophie Flouquet, Patrice Goulet,
Frederic Migayrou, and Philippe Trétiack,
and, of course, Églée, Aïna, and Basile.

Translated from the French by DAVID RADZINOWICZ
Copyediting: HELEN WOODHALL
Design: FRANÇOIS HUERTAS
Typesetting: THIERRY RENARD
Proofreading: CHRISOULA PETRIDIS
Color Separation: REPROSCAN
Printed in Slovenia by KOROTAN

Distributed in North America by Rizzoli International Publications, Inc.

Originally published in French as *Architecture Contemporaine: Mode d'Emploi*
© Flammarion, S. A., Paris, 2009

English-language edition
© Flammarion, S. A., Paris, 2010

10 11 12 3 2 1
ISBN: 978-2-08-030131-4
Dépôt légal: 03/2010